Tokujin Yoshioka Design

Survey by Ryu Niimi

Contributions by Elisa Astori, Issey Miyake,
Ross Lovegrove, Ingo Maurer, Paola Antonelli
and Kozo Fujimoto

Foreword

Driade and Tokujin Yoshioka
Elisa Astori

Tokujin Yoshioka came to furniture design through art and fashion. A set designer and creator of installations, he began collaborating with Driade in 2002 with his intense experiments in the application of unusual, lightweight materials such as paper to the furniture-design repertoire. Reinterpreting thousand-year-old Japanese crafts in an unusual iconographic and functional manner, he brought oriental accents to the field of international design, and a fresh approach to its technological and industrial potential. The results revealed the dream-like, secret dimension hidden behind the prosaicness of 'things'.

Driade is an aesthetic workshop, conducting research into home and lifestyle solutions and evolving, through different histories, around a single central nucleus. Founded in 1968 by a group comprised of Adelaide Acerbi and Antonia and Enrico Astori, the firm has achieved success due to the quality of its original ideas and its highly innovative manufacturing policy. Today, the vast Driade catalogue includes art objects and products for daily use, furniture for the home, garden and office, cabinets, kitchens and modular furniture systems.

Tokujin's Driade debut in 2002 with the highly successful range of furniture, Tokyo-pop, confirms how experimentation with new shapes and home-living ideas continues to constitute the company's vital core. Beginning with an armchair prototype, Honey-pop (2001), which was originally made by hand through a revolutionary use of paper, he worked out other seating elements, to be produced in rotational plastic, whose organic shapes stem exactly from the imprint left by the body when seated. The Tokyo-pop group of furniture includes a sofa, armchair, chaise-longue, high table and stools. Tokujin's masterful presentation of Honey-pop and Tokyo-pop in the dadriade showroom in Milan prompted critics to hail the birth of a new star in the design world.

The Tokujin-Driade collaboration on this project shows how the designer can be seen as the mother, and the company, the father, in the process of conceiving and developing a product. Driade transformed Tokujin's design into an industrial product, making it replicable in series by meticulously transposing the shape proposed by the artist into rotational plastic technology for large-scale manufacture. Today Tokyo-pop is an icon of the Driade collection, and Honey-pop is in the collections of the Museum of Modern Art, New York, the Vitra Design Museum, Berlin, the Centre Georges Pompidou, Paris, and the Victoria and Albert Museum, London.

Following this success, Driade commissioned Tokujin to conceive Clouds, a show held at the Rotonda della Besana in Milan in 2003, celebrating Driade's thirty-five years on the design scene. In the spacious bays of the church Rotonda in the ancient San Michele complex, Tokujin created a sort of surreal 'life in the clouds', in which History was presented as a 'field of miracles': a meadow evanescent with mist and decorated with the leaves and corollas of gaudy artificial flowers. Through these mists of memory, the visitor could glimpse fragments and outlines of the objects that have marked Driade's contribution to the iconography of the past three decades. Visual projections and refined lettering emphasized the salient moments of the various chapters in the company's long history.

In his furniture designs, Tokujin experiments with a sophisticated play of materials and shapes, and the freshness and creativity of his approach continues to amaze. Such organic sculptural forms and delight in transparency and the play of light are elements found, for example, in the Kiss Me Goodbye chair, presented in 2004, whose sinuous body is made of clear polycarbonate. For Tokujin, 'design' means communicating something fascinating, surprising, joyful, unexpected. His seemingly simple creations conceal many levels of profound meaning and are the result of meticulous thought processes aimed at transferring his ethereal poetic intuition into a final product with clear and functional use. It is for such contributions to the design world that we celebrate the work and vision of Tokujin.

Introduction

Yoshioka-kun and I
Issey Miyake

Tokujin Yoshioka joined the Miyake Design Studio in 1988, the year we started experimenting with pleats. At that time I was waging an inner struggle. Ever since the shock of the May Revolutions of 1968 in Paris, I had resolved to find a solution to clothing that would respond to the needs of people's daily lives: clothing for the many, rather than the few. However, I felt somewhat lost, buried in the deep forest that is the closed system of couture, with its long history and traditions. So I made a big decision – to take a leap forward with a new team. I consulted my friend, the late furniture designer Shiro Kuramata, since I was looking for someone whose viewpoint would come from outside the field of fashion. He introduced me to Yoshioka-kun, who had recently joined his office, and was generous enough to suggest that he joined us.

As Yoshioka-kun became more accustomed to working at the design studio, we gave him the job of creating the hats and other accessories used for the show. He immediately displayed a strong and individual aesthetic, as well as a talent for execution. He had an intuitive understanding of the balance, movement and sensibilities of the human body, even though he had received no formal training in this area. He was always on the hunt for interesting materials. I would say to myself, 'I haven't seen Yoshioka-kun for a few days', and then he would suddenly show up with something beautiful. In this search for materials, he would skim the surface of a pond, lightly and unhindered like a water boatman; and at the end he would always amaze us all.

I later put him in charge of window displays at our boutiques. Immediately, he started to present idea after idea, which attracted a great deal of attention from passers-by. He would make them smile and feel good, sometimes simply by creating a breeze using an electric

Opposite and right: Issey Miyake Making Things, touring exhibition, 1998–2000, the Ace Gallery, New York

Far right: Issey Miyake, window installation, 1998, Aoyama

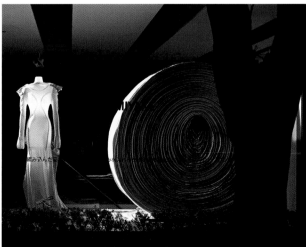

fan. This ability to create something that moves us, using simple tools, is at the root of his talent; he is superbly gifted in capturing people's hearts in this way. I believe that he is at his best when he makes skilful use of air, light and sometimes even gravity, rather than the use of concrete forms.

Some of our best-known collaborations are the work we have done for exhibitions. It all started with Energieen at the Stedelijk Museum in Amsterdam in 1990. I was one of fifteen contemporary artists in the exhibition, which also included Ettore Sottsass, Robert Wilson, Anselm Kiefer and Cindy Sherman. Their work was deemed to radiate energy. I worked with Yoshioka-kun, discussing many ideas, and moving towards a solution through a process of trial and error, as to how to exhibit a group of pleated dresses that I had created entitled Rhythm Pleats, inspired by the paintings of Henri Rousseau

(1844–1910). The pleated dresses were filled with air and modelled on mannequins or were displayed as pleated squares, rounds and ovals, flat on the floor. The viewers had to take off their shoes to walk around the exhibition. Even this small detail heightened their awareness and sense of touch; one feels warmth as the soles of one's feet touch the ground while walking around; there is a heightened sense of motion and tactility. This was very successful, not only as a way in which to view the exhibited items but also, as a way to experience the exhibition using all one's senses.

It is fun working with Yoshioka-kun. We have many discussions and I have learned that I can always expect to be surprised. He consistently responds to my requests with brilliance and his results never fail to astonish his viewers. He has created many of his own pieces as well, including the Honey-pop chair (2001), and he has

Right: Energieen, exhibition, 1990,
Stedelijk Museum, Amsterdam

Right: Silicon Hat, 1991, accessories for
the Issey Miyake Paris collection

developed a new and unique method of working, which I am thrilled to watch.

One of the most interesting aspects of Yoshioka-kun's work, and another of his abilities, is that by the time of its completion he has totally erased his own imprint from his work. No one, seeing one of his finished pieces, ever has a sense of his having been a part of it. This also applies to the man himself. By the time a piece or installation is completed it is too late to ask 'Where is Yoshioka-kun?', because he has already gone off elsewhere, moving in a new direction and involved in new projects and places.

In 1998, ten years after my turning point, I took on yet another new challenge: A-POC (A Piece Of Cloth). I embarked on this adventure with a new team of young designers including Dai Fujiwara. Yoshioka-kun had left our Studio by then and had become independent, involving himself with many new people and

broadening the scope of his work. Happily, however, we continue to collaborate with him.

With his enthusiasm and vigour, it is impossible to predict just how far he may push himself in the future. I am sure that even by the time this book comes out, he will have found new ways with which to thrill us. I look forward to his future surprises with anticipation.

Right: Issey Miyake Twist, exhibition, 1992, Benesse House Naoshima Contemporary Art Museum

Above: Issey Miyake Double Image,
window installation, 1999, Aoyama

Below: L'eau d'Issey Pour Homme,
window installation, 1995, Aoyama

Survey

A Poetics of the Totality
of Existence
Ryu Niimi

Tokujin Yoshioka, born 1967, is one of the most radical of today's Japanese designers, celebrated both in his own country and internationally. Looking back over his astonishing career, one becomes highly aware of the tremendous integrity of his designs, the almost obsessive consistency with which they remain true to a sense of universal totality, never succumbing to fragmentation. He sees materials as a kind of fluid body from which all the other elements of the design emerge, in one movement, one moment, one surface. Tokujin opens up the material world to find within it fruitful meanings for our lives.

Avoiding the modern concept of 'design' or even 'anti-design', Tokujin always situates himself beyond borders where he can be led, instead, by the interpretation of objects through the thick sensuality of the material and

its shadow-world of imagery and conceptual metaphysics. Without a strategy, his work is a natural extension of the character of a unique man whose designs never fail to ask the question 'what is design?' within their existence. Through such an approach, his work is forever an open-system, where the material is something that grows, happens and transforms again through tactile contact with our bodies. In this way, a simple object such as a chair becomes an intriguing living system.

It is for such reasons that whenever I am faced with the work of Tokujin I cannot help recalling the legendary Marcel Duchamp (1887–1968), especially in the context of his mystical project and concept of 'infra-mince'. In their enigmatic roles, both are artists who exist as a hinge between two worlds, which touch and intersect

Below left: Tokujin, 2001, at the Vitra
Design Museum, Berlin

Below right: Tokujin at the Hermès new
watch Dressage installation, 2003,
Koishikawa Annex University Museum,
University of Tokyo

each other from both sides, crossing over between the visible and the invisible, the body and the machine, the material and the visionary worlds.

If one can attempt to find a definition for Tokujin's designs, there are some specific factors that can be considered. He adores 'thinness', to try and combine an object into a whole through the act of transparency, so that the material speaks in its most simple, bare form, and thus expresses its own integrity. It is an expression that has also found continuity in his work for exhibition installations, where the integrity of the space becomes dependent on how it is received by the viewer, through its tactile properties. Whether objects, installations or 'happenings', the key inspiration always remains how the act of design is expressed and experienced. In his own words, Tokujin reaches for the 'point zero' of design.

Shunning rupture and discontinuity, he wishes everything to be unbroken, uninterrupted, and by the same token, he vigorously challenges the limitations of territorialism, preferring the universal. This holistic approach runs opposite to the contemporary paradigm of multiplicity; Tokujin's dream comes closer to a more idealistic idea of a community-oriented society. His work manifests a strong spirit of protest against our consumer-oriented society, and the forceful appearance of totality and integrity in his design can be read as part of this campaign against the fragmented character of the modern world. Thus, he takes a philosophical, even ethical, approach to design and its context.

This fundamental interplay of society and design runs the gamut from heavy-duty industrial mass production to personal, made-to-measure interior and exhibition spaces. Tokujin creates objects that fundamentally question their own role and identity, and he loves to present the process of design as an inspiring 'happening'. This term derives from the social-protest or nonsense-oriented performances by avant-garde artists during the 1960s, and although Tokujin is understated and reticent by nature, like these artists, he is a true radical. His radicalism does not stem from a superficial political attitude, but from his respect for the daily lives of ordinary people. He calls passionately for an alternative way of living, appreciating and producing things, and eschews many of the elements that are related to a conservative approach to design: consumerism, self-conscious 'style', the thematic or pedagogical, and so on.

While he has sometimes stated that he thinks of his design as being like Japanese cuisine, because the complicated process and the huge expenditure of time and effort leading up to it are belied by the extremely simple result he achieves, for him, designing is not just about creating beautiful or stylish objects. It is about reviving social processes and human communication. This places him within the specific genealogy of socially-engaged designers of the past. He can be compared, for example, to William Morris, and the anonymous, socially-oriented design Tokujin espouses, as well as his emphasis on a marriage between function and exquisite craftsmanship, constitutes a revival of the nineteenth-century Arts and Crafts Movement that was instituted in post-war industrial Japan by Sori Yanagi.

This revival echoed the aesthetic exchange that had taken place between European and Japanese art and design at the turn of the century. The Japonisme movement was prevalent throughout Europe, and dominated the consciousness of artists, designers and architects who were seeking new ideas and forms for modern design that would break away from historicism and conservative, ornamental approaches. They found the key in the works of Japanese artists, who were embracing the natural world as a source for their designs, forms and colours. Thus Japonisme fed into and became incorporated within the general wave of Art Nouveau, which has now come full circle with Tokujin's organic works.

Thinness, transparency, material integrity: these words recall the mainstream Modernist design tradition. They could equally be applied, for example, to the works of the Art Nouveau designer of the Glasgow School, Charles Rennie Mackintosh, at the beginning of the twentieth century. His uninterrupted, organic shapes, where visible form is always closely tied to material sensuality, are reminiscent of Tokujin's designs. However, Mackintosh's sensuality derives from the Modernist strategy of deconstructing volume and mass, while

Tokujin is more concerned with bringing together everyday materials with environmental reflection and mass production. One could also link Tokujin's work to the mid-century organic and biomorphic design of Charles Eames, George Nelson, Alexander Girard and Arne Jacobsen. But however much Tokujin admires these great forerunners, he has led post-war design towards a different phase.

Stylistically speaking, it is difficult to place Tokujin within any particular contemporary design trend. His brand of material sensuality is rare in today's design world, where for example the theatrical, playful approach of Philippe Starck offers a flamboyant and decadent design, or the visual spectacle of Fabio Novembre's interiors can seem merely ornamental. These design strategies have never occurred in Tokujin's ethical philosophy. He does not play with gesture or pretence. To this extent his can be seen as a Zen-style practice, with an oriental restraint and simple humbleness. The different types of material sensations that his work elicits are closely related to his penetrating perspective on daily products and materials. It is not aesthetic gestures, but faith in the interactive relationship between human beings and materials that motivates his designs. One can see something similar to this sincere character in the work of Jasper Morrison perhaps, who also expresses an honest approach towards everyday existence in his designs.

Right: Tokujin's homage to Marcel Breuer's classic chair, produced in 1989 at the age of twenty-two, using liquid crystal EL

Far right: Martini glass for Bombay Sapphire, 2003

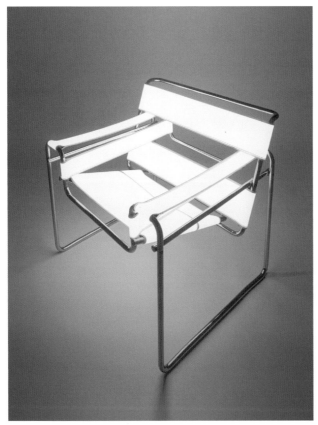

Below left: EL Table, an early design
adopting the liquid crystal EL, 1990

Below middle: Apple, presentation
plan, 1997

Below right: BMW, installation,
1998, Tokyo

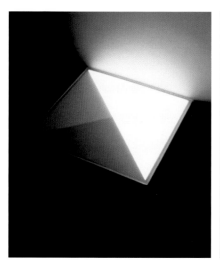

A more convincing genealogy, however, can be traced from Tokujin's master, the late Shiro Kuramata, to his more recent collaborator Issey Miyake. After graduating from a course in Industrial Design at Kuwasawa Design School in 1986, Tokujin worked in Kuramata's office for a short period (1987–8). His mentor's lifelong passion for lightness and transparency in design has found its way into Tokujin's work, and is especially evident in his determination to conceal the physical structure and support systems in his furniture. He has also inherited Kuramata's playful, entertaining spirit, which renders the objects of both designers similar to artworks. This is not to say that they are obsessed with the original, one-off object, but that they are interested in creating fantastic and imaginative products that have a powerful effect on the emotions, whilst never losing their footing in the requirements of daily life.

Tokujin first began to really make his mark while working with Issey Miyake on the design of accessories such as hats and bags for the Paris Collections, and he continues to collaborate with him on a series of ground-breaking

exhibition and shop designs. In these interiors, Tokujin mobilizes every factor in the space until it becomes so dense that it achieves a bodily tactility. In Miyake's A-POC (A Piece Of Cloth) shop in Aoyama (2000), Tokujin produced such an effect, as if the shop were wearing the industrial material with which it was clad throughout. A-POC was Miyake's watershed in brand production, using a new industrial process to make clothes in a single piece. Tokujin applied this concept to the interior, adapting technology from automobile exhaust panels, and using recycled, one-piece moulded aluminium. He created a space with an unprecedented materiality, combining industrial speed with the intimacy of the craftsman's work. 'I always want to bring something into being that I have never seen, but yearn to see', he has said. His impressive interpretation of A-POC's 'industrial-wear' concept realized a spectacular play on the idea of wear-space/space-wear without resorting to crude visual trickery. Material and sensuality are similarly combined into one, non-hierarchical body in the interior design for the Issey Miyake shop (2001) in Kobe. Here, Tokujin realized a highly sensual space by means of a combination of materials and light through moving images, creating a multi-layered and overlapping set of contrasts and gradations, defined by Tokujin as a 'novel transparency'.

In Tokujin's first great touring show, Issey Miyake Making Things (1998–2000), for which he made use of garment-hanging machines and various floor projections, he clearly demonstrates the approach he takes in his designs for exhibitions. He repeatedly creates a 'ground material' with which to communicate the theme of the overall installation – the process of making clothes and projection of moving images. Gradually, sensually, almost unconsciously, viewers become aware of these materials, which draw them in to a novel sphere of communication. Thus Tokujin achieves an open process where space goes beyond materials. The experience is akin to being placed inside a new discovery zone, a shadow of the visible world, or a fourth dimension.

In the exhibition, Robot Meme, held at the National Museum of Emerging Science and Innovation, Tokyo, in 2001, he showed his talent in handling permeable and membrane-like forms, excelling with objects and spaces in which shadows and colours intertwine. This show comprised a huge, winding transparent wall made up of embossed human body shapes, modelled in

polycarbonate. Occupying with one's sensual body the territory between these transparent bodies, which were reminiscent of recycled water bottles and other everyday materials, visitors were reported to have experienced a gorgeous dizzy feeling. Tokujin achieved this out-of-body sensation by opening up a new form of communication that made use of the interaction between the human memory of materials and an awareness of one's own physical body. Similarly, his breathtaking interior for Think Zone (2001), an experimental art project in Tokyo conceived in collaboration with Bruce Mau, appealed to all five senses at once in a design that integrated all its elements into a vast, single entity. Here, images were projected onto the floor, which in turn would seem to float when viewed from the street outside through a glass wall.

One can predict that Tokujin's approach to design will make the same kind of impact on the new generation of world-wide designers as that exerted by Miyake, who has acted as an icon for the post-war international fashion and design culture. Both Miyake and Tokujin share a Zen-inspired philosophy in which all things are one body and nothing can be separated. For both, design is not just about the fabrication of material, but something that grows with use. Tokujin has since branched out into new collaborations, which have included spacial designs for NTT-X (2000), Audi (2001) and Peugeot (2004), as well as interior living spaces

Below: Preparations for Issey Miyake Making Things, touring exhibition, 1998–2000, the Ace Gallery, New York

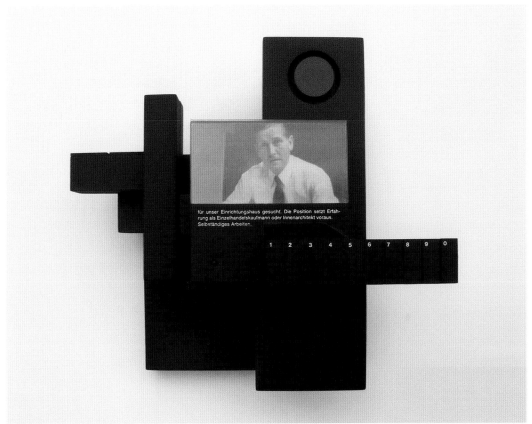

for Muji (2003), where the focus has continued to be on sensory experience. But it is in establishing his own company, Tokujin Yoshioka Design, in 2000, that his approach is most telling. In choosing the location for his office, he decided to physically move a vernacular building, a 150-year-old rice barn in Shimane, truss by truss, to transform it into a new studio space in Tokyo. Once again, he found a way to bring the traditional into his ever-changing new world.

The distinctiveness of Tokujin's work also derives from a determination to challenge stereotypes. He poses the question that should be asked by every designer: what does design offer beyond the harmonious use of materials, form and colour? His products encapsulate both question and answer in their design. Whether an installation, an object or an interior, the end result is deceptively simple, giving little indication of the highly conceptual nature of the design process. His materials always remain true to the concept, since it is his philosophy never to infringe on their autonomous, self-sufficient territory – a view based on a wider, pragmatic attitude to the environment, its users and everyone who comes into contact with his work. Even from his early projects, such as the Bared Flashlight (1985), Tokujin found his expression in the search for the essence of things, as the light bears the natural form of its function.

Above left: TV Phone, 1986

Above right: Bared Flashlight, 1985

The notion of transformation through the sensual tactility of our bodies, a dominant theme in his interior work, soon found expression in another product, Tokujin's revolutionary Honey-pop (2001) chair. It was this project that was later developed by Driade into the precast plastic Tokyo-pop range of seating (2002). Made up of a honeycomb structure of thin layers of glassine paper, Honey-pop comes flat-packed until it is opened out into a 3-D form, whose process is then completed by the weight and body shape of the user. When Tokujin put the prototype on display, viewers were fascinated to see a new material being born in front of them. With Honey-pop, he transformed the mundane chair into an intriguing, living system; an isolated material into a fascinating and moving entity; the man-material relationship into a more vital poetics. This drastic shift in the concept of a chair into a lightweight material-system represents the essence of his work. Its dramatic elegance and organic sensuality, its concept of one body, one surface, places it on a par, for example, with the work of architect Frank Gehry.

In the lighting system, TōFU (2000), the first of Tokujin's designs to be commercially produced, the materials are a kind of body from which the elements of the design emerge with great freedom and clarity, as a kind of surprise, but always controlled by their function and concept, in this case a simple food ingredient. With this product, he could be credited as the first designer successfully to overcome the division between the fixture and the light source. 'This is not a design that comes from deploying lighting fixtures', he said, 'it comes from light itself'.

His aim to return to a 'zero-point', pursuing design to its deepest origins, has tempered his work into something super-direct and super-primitive. But if it is true to say that his design is not sophisticated or refined, must we conclude that he is less a designer than an artist? In the sense that he has achieved uniqueness in his work, one could indeed compare him to a contemporary artist. However, the strict challenge he sets himself is to stick to the basic concept of 'things for everybody'. And these 'things for everybody' must be new things for everybody. But how does one make everyday things new? How does one review and look at them from a fresh perspective, given their strong history and place in the cultural memory?

The answer may lie in a fundamental truth that Tokujin learned from another great icon of the twentieth century, the great American-Japanese artist Isamu Noguchi (1904–88): that any creator attempting to discover a new art for the people should recall and communicate previous models. Making his name during the late-1930s as a leading sculptor in New York, Noguchi also worked throughout his career with various overlapping genres, including works in stone, clay, paper, earth, as well as stage design, architecture and interior-product design, creating elegant abstract environments. But the characteristic typology of his work was open, communicative and collaborative. Following World War II, he dramatically reinvented his career, travelling round Europe and Asia and studying the prehistoric ruins, temples and landmarks, with the purpose of creating landscape-architecture-sculpture projects that would provide a new model for communal public spaces. He believed that sculpture should not just adorn rich people's houses, or even museums, but that its modern role was to serve the public as religious architecture had done before

Below left: Honey-pop, chair, 2001, Tokujin Yoshioka Design

Below right: Tokujin working on the design for the Tokyo-pop, 2002, Driade

Above: Tokujin in his Tokyo office

it. This has inspired Tokujin's designs for the twenty-first century: 'things for everyone, things for human dreams'.

The genealogy between them is best explained through the Chair That Disappears in the Rain (2003), designed by Tokujin in homage to Noguchi, as a means of imagining what this great figure would be creating were he born one hundred years from now. The material, optical glass, with its immaterial structure references Noguchi's interest in 'form beyond form', with which he experimented in all kinds of materials and genres throughout his lifetime. The project, in which this transparent experience of a chair was placed in Roppongi Hills, Tokyo, was created as a streetscape happening for passers-by. Through this gesture, Tokujin was declaring himself a disciple of the man who dreamt of 'sculpting the air itself'. This theme of transparency has continued in other works, such as Kiss Me Goodbye (2004), which is more of an essence of than a real chair.

Today, Tokujin continues not only to astound but to also find new pathways and directions. Materials still lead the way, whether it be the Boing chair with its pleated leather textile, the simplicity of the TO watch, or the play of light achieved through glass and fibre optics in the Stardust chandelier for crystal-manufacturer Swarovski (all 2005). Perhaps there will also be a realization of the Transparent Kura project, a concept for a see-through garage with glass walls and roof tiles. Tokujin has himself confessed a recent interest in various kinds of fibres, for example, which are sure to surface in some product

or place in the future in a way that the audience can come alive through the five senses of the body as well as through an awakening of the mind.

The attempt to achieve a single body of transparency might sum up Tokujin's work. He aims for the point where the material world both appears and vanishes. He does not see design as an opaque or closed-system of mere production, but as a two-way resource with which to add meaning to our lives. While the next generation will surely be hugely inspired by his works, they will have much to live up to when following in the wake of this futuristic and enigmatic animist. More than any other designer or architect, Tokujin Yoshioka has brought about a rebirth in material design.

Transparency

Otherworldliness
Ross Lovegrove

Anish Kapoor, the great contemporary British sculptor, has said that almost every day he reads and re-reads from the same book: *A Zen Harvest* by Soiku Shigematsu. As I travel in South-east Asia at the time of writing this essay, I too read and re-read from a book as a constant companion. Written by Dore Ashton it is called *East and West*, and it is about the life and work of Isamu Noguchi.

I bought it on 19 July 1996 in Long Island City and even as I revisit the book, whatever the world I might be navigating at the time, I find the words ever more appropriate and enriching. There is one particular sentence written by Martha Graham that refers to Noguchi's work as having something of a strange beauty and 'otherworldliness' and when I read this I often think of Tokujin Yoshioka.

I say this not because of the concept of strange beauty, which for me is often a result of innovative thinking or experiencing something beyond one's everyday aesthetic condition, but because the word 'otherworldliness' contains a vision that is beyond the everyday or banal, and takes our mind into a realm of beauty that is emotionally all-encompassing.

Tokujin's solutions are drawn from silent contemplation and from a unique ability to visualize spaces, objects and light. He can sense and manipulate the richness of changing perspectives to such an acute degree in his mind's eye that the actual three-dimensional results are strikingly sensual and atmospheric. This imagination and precision of planning is a singular activity that gives nothing away until the final making and installation of the piece. In this regard Tokujin works as a true artist: one can never see or imagine from his private process the absolute impact of his ideas until they become physical. In this, our eternal silent relationship, lies a mutual ground where we meet to exchange ideas, and there is the frequent surprise of the new: what is that structure? What is that material? I've never seen that process before. Can I touch it? Where is it from? Did you make it? How are you going to use it?

In a world that is becoming increasingly homogeneous and monotonous, Tokujin's work inspires a value system that unites art, design and 'materialism'. This is a new condition and one that benefits from the core of his culture and his own awareness of its significance. This 'Japaneseness' can be seen and felt in the work of many contemporaries such as Kazuo Sejima, Shigeru Ban, Toyo Ito, and continues in the work of the Miyake Design Studio, for example. What appears to characterize the work of such artists is their sincere appreciation of materials and the economy of their use as structure and surface. Such structures, expressed as surface skin, thin, light and paper-like in their simple geometries, are revealed for example in the use of the white paper model in the work of SANAA, or the direct way that tubes are placed vertically or joined with wooden blocks in the highly individual work of Shigeru Ban.

However, today there is more than ever a global consciousness between many artists, architects and designers who, although living and working in different cultures share the same spirit of invention with materials and processes. This awareness is in itself uplifting and creates a united force of uniqueness that is integral to the process of creativity, encouraged through the ease of travel that can bring these minds closer together. Tokujin's new-found access to Europe is a recent phenomenon, but his work has brought with it a new spirit, which communicates a sincerity of thought process through pieces that we could never have anticipated or experienced before. This is for many a liberating moment of innovation, both physically and intellectually, because Tokujin's work lives outside the boundaries of plagiaristic commercial repetition, but within its own sphere of relevance. Again one awaits with great anticipation his new designs for Yamagiwa, Driade and others because they follow a new individual path that breathes a new life into the culture of manufacturing, which lies somewhere between high technology and high craft. This innate ability to translate progressive thoughts into progressive aesthetic solutions is more akin to the process of an artist rather than a designer and this is what elevates his work beyond the popular or banal. There is something spiritual in the way he approaches material mass, bringing it lightness and transparency.

When I recall great works of art or design that have truly moved me, I cannot forget the astonishing beauty of Robot Meme as I saw it installed at the National Museum of Emerging Science and Innovation, Tokyo, in 2001. It was for me an atmospheric phenomenon, since the curtain of lightweight, vacuum-formed sheets depicting the human body was held so effortlessly in space. What moved me then and still moves me today was the delicate interplay of material and light, capturing a magical sense of volume invisibly constructed from a minimal material, for a maximum polysensorial effect. Tokujin's silent understanding of material processes displays a rare intuition, but in his hands the concept of transparency and light is always communicated in an optimal form that combines logic and beauty. The logic is present because the clarity of communication is immediately perceived, and the beauty is present because of the spectacular effect it has on our sense of space.

Somehow, I never feel that there is any pretence or calculation in Tokujin's work; it presents itself with spontaneity and as an instinctive reflex to a situation – spontaneity, meticulously constructed, one could say. His design for Issey Miyake's A-POC (A Piece of Cloth) Namba space in Osaka (2001) achieved this with a special convergence of functional elements, dominated by bubbles, which introduced light into the space during the day and projected it out at night. These large, blown, acrylic bubbles also created an air of insulation and with it a futuristic atmosphere that I found light and engaging without ever feeling it was 'designed' in the way that many commercial spaces try too hard to be. In this sense he plays with our notion of permanence and impermanence. His work for Miyake, even if intended to be temporary as an exhibition space or window design, remains etched on one's mind; the senses are deeply touched and thus the memory is retained.

Tokujin's ongoing works are becoming ever more thoughtful and technological through his high level of perception and subtle method of enquiry; he begins with an innate ability to reduce an idea to its essence without his work feeling repetitive or formulaic. For me, his emphasis on aura adheres to an organic principle of truth to materials, letting them guide his creativity, and in the very natural way he dematerializes mass through transparency.

As he has taken this instinct for transparency and optical beauty into the world of furniture, Tokujin has once again proved that his silent study of the problem can give rise to totally original, totally unforeseen results that move people from within. His work, for example, with optical, telescopic grade glass in his furniture for Mori in Roppongi Hills, Tokyo, called Chair That

Disappears in the Rain (2003), is a modern masterpiece that brings high art into the realm of everyday life. Surprisingly, however valuable the raw material might be, its recomposition and modelling has made it accessible to the man on the street, which is a testimony to Tokujin's natural, non-elitist generosity of ideas. Similarly, the use of the pure geometries in the TO watch project (2005), a new timepiece for Issey Miyake, takes an object of daily use and introduces a universal language to it. An accessible art form that reaches another world whose main attraction is newness, originality, and high art and semi-rarity. It can be understood and read directly without education, without complex instruction but is born out of a very unique cultural platform that has been reduced to its purist expression.

There are a few silent affinities that traverse both our worlds and this is one of the special reasons why I feel such a powerful empathy with Tokujin and his work. Today, as we see industrial companies responding to his vision in other countries, the results are inspiring cultural and commercial success across an increasing broad spectrum of consumer products. This is a natural path for Tokujin. Works such as the TōFU lamp (2000) or the Tokyo-pop (2002) and Kiss Me Goodbye (2004) chairs have the legitimacy, like those of Issey Miyake and Tadao Ando, for example, to traverse worlds and to bring with them a highly sophisticated view of transparency and its impact on our perception of space and living in the modern world.

Ultimately, Tokujin's work represents a freedom of expression because his eye for the unique, and his self-awareness of his abilities are, in many ways, a natural editing process that eliminates banality and gravitates towards the unknown. This is the 'otherworldliness' I refer to, the aura of expectation and the result that is an expression of his philosophy.

We have entered a third millennium dominated by science, biology and new ways of thinking. Now that we are here we need to evolve processes and attitudes, which reflect our artistic potential; we are all different, with different influences and expectations and we thrive on the infinity of ideas and the absolute beauty of a creativity that is well defined and well expressed. In a world that is growing exponentially, surprise, insight, stimulation and sincerity will help us retain our vision, and Tokujin belongs to a new breed of designer-artist that will help us communicate the spirituality of physical existence, translating abstract technologies into objects of desire and intelligence.

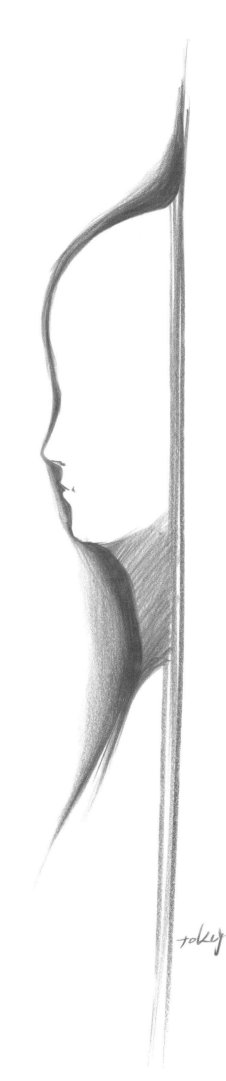

Robot Meme

For this exhibition, Tokujin filled the space with 700
transparent 'bodies' created out of injected polycarbonate
to evoke a futuristic robot factory. Robots, born out of the human
imagination and created through the power of science, are
also 'babies' on their way to growing into 'adult humans'.
Tokujin interpreted the theme by using the concept of the
'human body' as the ultimate robot design, incorporating
all kinds of functions.

Robot Meme, exhibition, 2001,
National Museum of Emerging Science
and Innovation, Tokyo

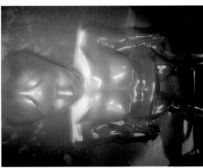

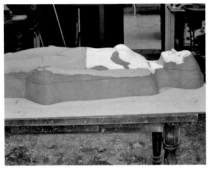

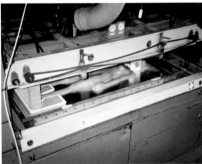

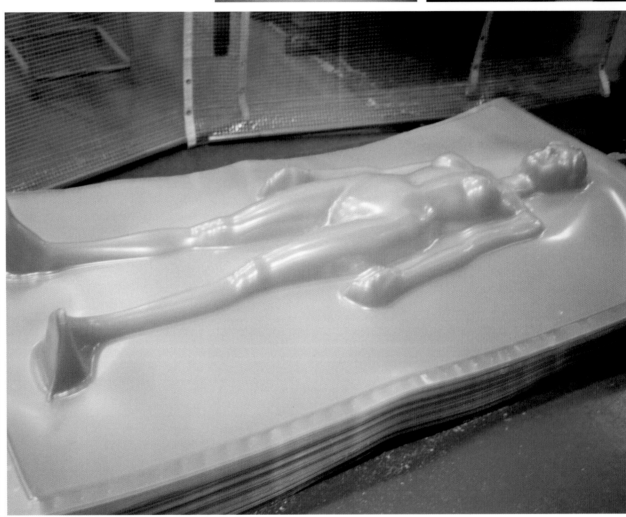

The manufacturing process involved creating human-shaped moulds which were injected with the polycarbonate and joined together in rows. In this way, identical life-size human figures were created and repeated in a process reminiscent of cloning.

Robot Meme, exhibition, 2001,
National Museum of Emerging Science
and Innovation, Tokyo

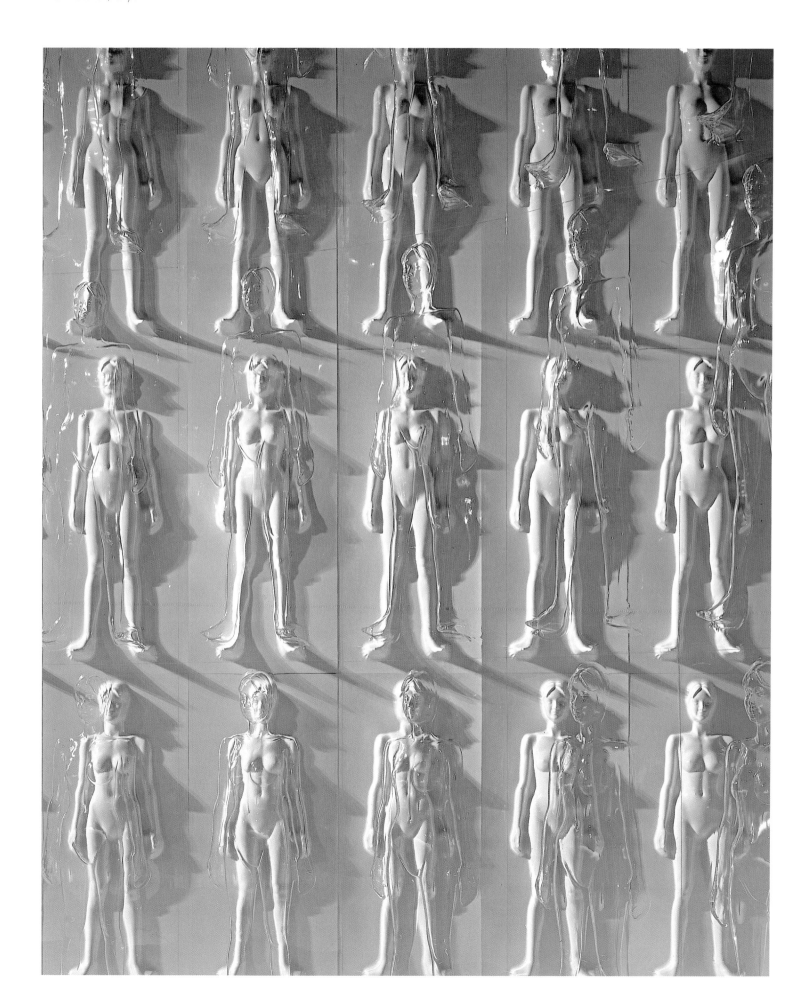

The display featured a series of curved, transparent
walls made up of the figures. Visitors walked between
them to engage in the disconcerting mirroring
experience of the space.

Robot Meme, exhibition, 2001,
National Museum of Emerging Science
and Innovation, Tokyo

Robot Meme, exhibition, 2001,
National Museum of Emerging Science
and Innovation, Tokyo

Think Zone

This project in Roppongi offers a new type of experimental
art. Stepping inside the 'zone', which also incorporates a cafe,
gallery and bookstore, the effect is that the future has arrived.
The space projects images onto the entire floor, which in turn,
when viewed from the street outside through a glass wall,
seems to float upwards.

Think Zone, architectural project, 2001,
Roppongi, Tokyo

Think Zone, architectural project, 2001,
Roppongi, Tokyo

Think Zone, architectural project, 2001,
Roppongi, Tokyo

The wall is made from a specially-manufactured optical glass,
developed by Tokujin, to achieve the required impact when
the building is viewed from the outside.

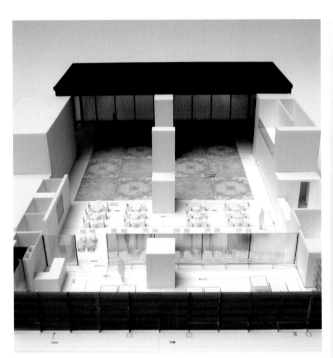

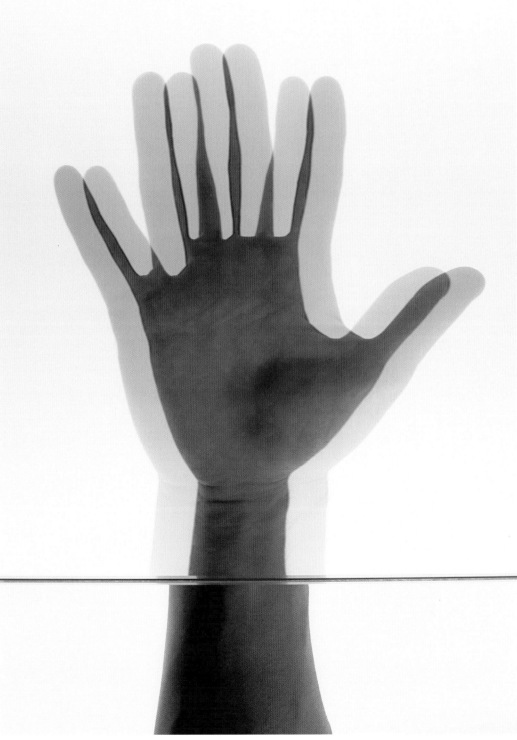

Think Zone, architectural project, 2001,
Roppongi, Tokyo

Issey Miyake – Taipei

For this shop interior, Tokujin plays with themes of transparency and double vision. Placing special optical glass in between the clothes on display and in stock, he brings into the open what is usually concealed from the customer and harmonizes both functions of the shop. The glass creates a world of fantasy, which blurs the boundary between reality and the future. Tokujin pursued a new interpretation of the interior space by incorporating the immediate communication between people and clothes into one of the core design elements, for the clothing line developed by Naoki Takizawa since 2000.

Issey Miyake, shop interior,
2004, Taipei

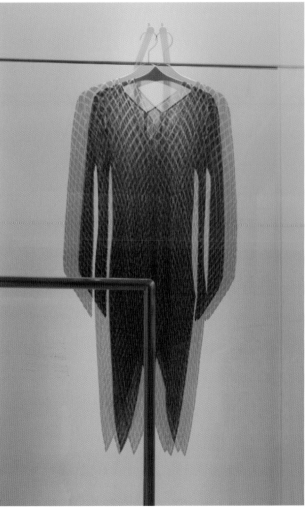

ISSEY MIYAKE

Chair That Disappears in the Rain

This is part of a streetscape project on permanent display
in the heart of Tokyo, which also features the work of eleven
designers from around the world, including Ron Arad,
Ettore Sottsass and Gijs Bakker. When it rains, Tokujin's chair
looks as if it is disappearing, just like the outline of a piece
of glass disappearing as it is dropped into water. The project
is inspired by the question, 'If Isamu Noguchi were alive 100
years from now, what would he make?'.

Chair That Disappears in the Rain, chair,
2003, Roppongi Hills, Tokyo

Chair That Disappears in the Rain, chair,
2003, Roppongi Hills, Tokyo

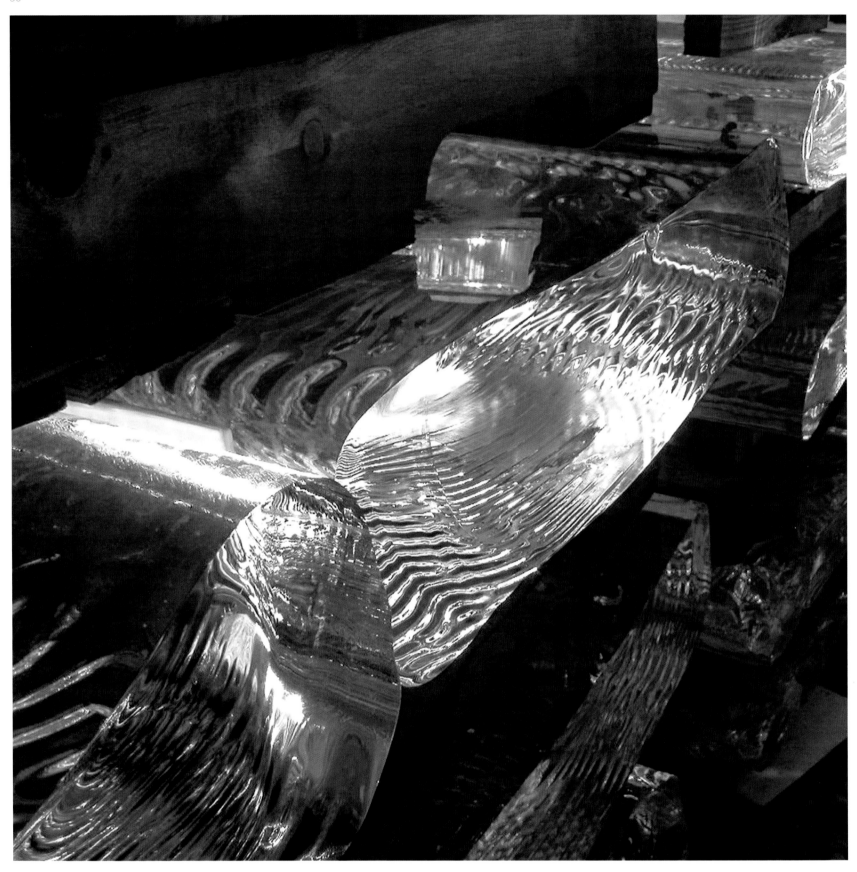

Chair That Disappears in the Rain, chair,
2003, Roppongi Hills, Tokyo

The chair is manufactured from the same material used in giant
observatory telescopes and crafted by special techniques.
Another chair carved out of a block of the same glass is placed
next to it.

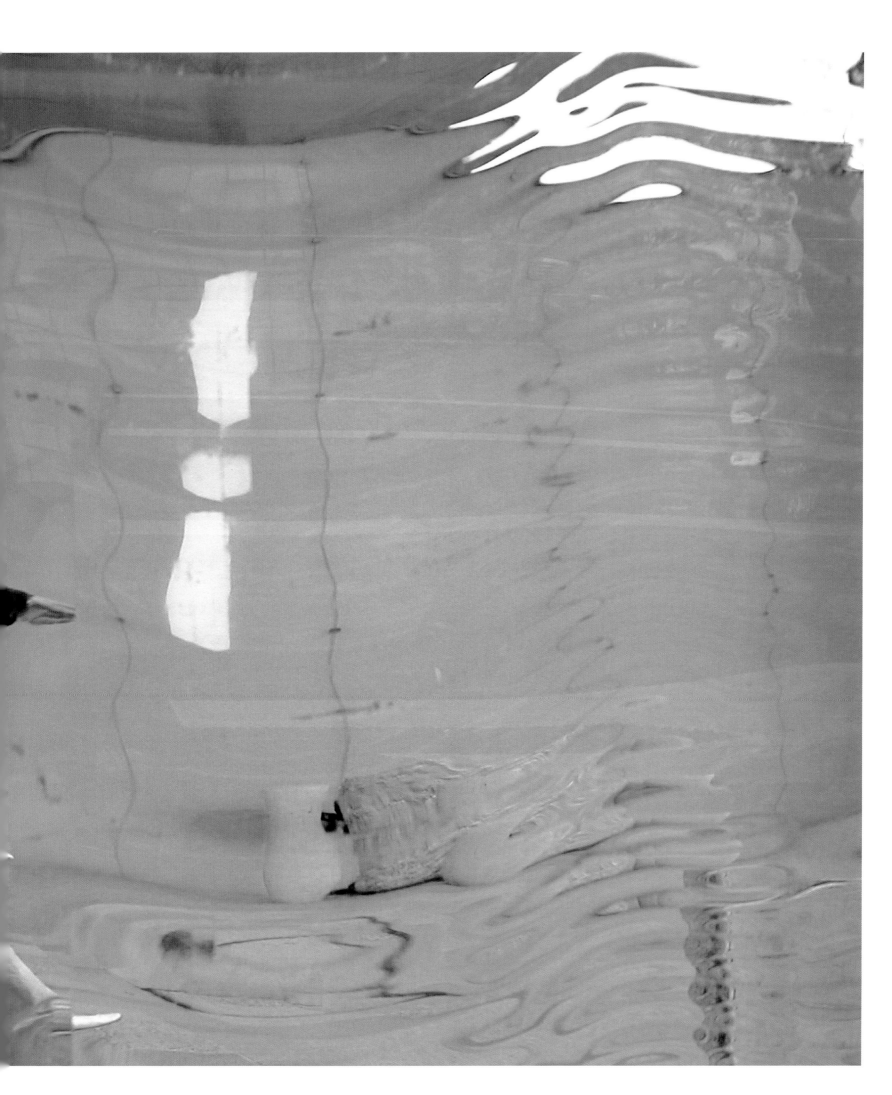

Chair That Disappears in the Rain, chair,
2003, Roppongi Hills, Tokyo

For Tokujin, it was important that the chair would provide a
meeting point for people passing by. Its descriptive name was
selected to make it an approachable and familiar object.

Kiss Me Goodbye

This chair is based on the concept of finding beauty in an object that is formless, that cannot be seen or touched, like perfume. The object is designed with a sense of transparency that is conceived through the notion of floating in a space without gravity.

Kiss Me Goodbye, chair,
2004, Driade

Kiss Me Goodbye, chair,
2004, Driade

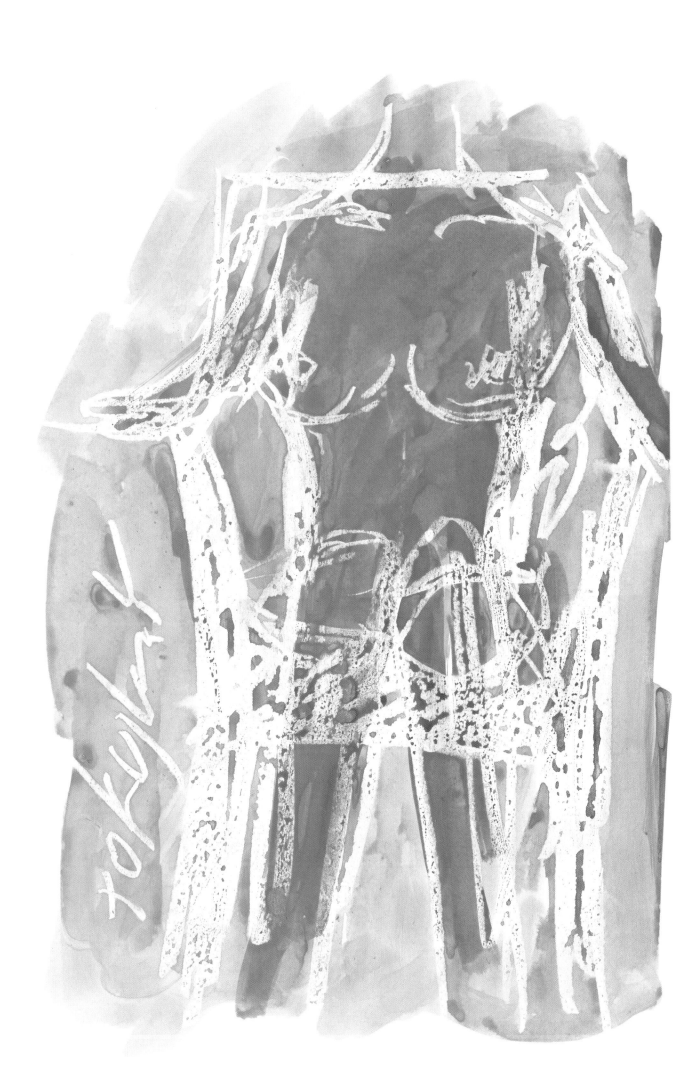

The design of the chair is inspired by an after-image of the sitter's body after they have just left. It plays with the idea of camouflage, representing the figure of a person who blends into the surrounding scenery and eventually becomes invisible. It is the result of an early concept by Tokujin, dating from as long ago as 1999.

Transparent Kura, architectural project,
ongoing, Kagoshima

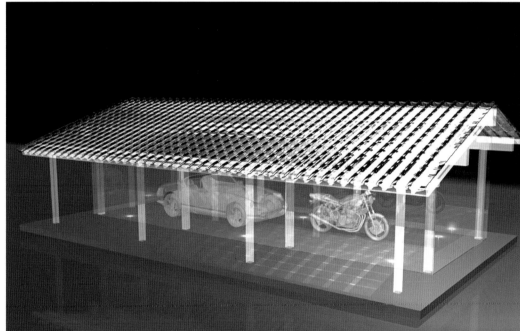

Transparent Kura

This is an architectural project to create a futuristic 'minka', or
Japanese private house. The concept is for the client to be able
to 'gaze at his cars as an element of everyday living' through
this transparent garage. It uses glass walls and glass 'kawara',
or roof tiles, that slot together and enclose the space.

Toyota

This design for a booth for Toyota expresses the concept of 'Vibrant Clarity' by featuring the optical reflector used in the rear lamp of a car to structure the total space. Using over 100,000 pieces of this material, the installation creates a magical effect as it plays with ideas of reflection that distort multiple images of cars upwards onto the walls.

Toyota, booth design, 2005,
Tokyo Motor Show

Toyota, booth design, 2005,
Tokyo Motor Show

Toyota, booth design, 2005,
Tokyo Motor Show

Motion

Reflective Movements
Ingo Maurer

Movement is one of the most basic elements of our lives. It takes so many different forms. When I was asked to write something on the subject and began to reflect on it, I thought of everyday, deliberate movements such as those of a dancer or someone working: movements that take place within our own bodies, or experiences of passive motion, such as sitting in a plane and being carried from one place to another. But there are also the movements we see as spectators: the bustle of traffic, the motion of trees, fish and birds, water and wind, as well as the movement of feelings, the emotions.

Ever since my first visit to Japan, I have been impressed by the continual movement everywhere in the cities, the activities of cars, trains and pedestrians, which operate with an intensity I have never seen in Europe or America. Streams of movement run across the city, following ordered paths that are purposeful and dynamic. I had the good fortune to be guided by a good friend who not only showed me new and interesting places but also sorted out everyday problems. During my first trip to Japan, in 1970 – when Tokujin was still a small boy – I had the opportunity to watch various craftsmen at work. Later I observed the artisans in Shikoku who were making fans for the collection we were producing at the time. Their movements made a very strong impression on me. They seem to follow different rules, quite distinct from European patterns of movement. It is hard to say exactly where the differences lie, but it is always a pleasure to watch a Japanese cook or a waitress – the very name seems wrong, here – or a street-cleaner or scaffolder. For Tokujin, himself a person who moves in a very calm, deliberate way, these things are part of the natural reality that he has known and absorbed since early childhood. Born in southern Japan, in Kyushu, he must have received impressions every day that would strike foreigners as unusual but were perfectly normal to him.

As well as these human movements, there are the natural types of motion that we notice as observers, enjoying or overlooking them according to our own receptivity. By this I mean, for example, the movement of leaves on a tree swaying in the wind, a flock of birds in flight, or the ripple of waves in open water. I grew up on the island of Reichenau on Lake Constance in Germany, which is full of vegetable gardens, with tall willow trees by the water's edge and small yachts and rowing boats on the lake. Light falls through the leaves as they dance above the shallow waves that slap over the gravel by the shore. Patches and points of light flicker endlessly back and forth. Children absorb impressions of this kind in an unconscious, spontaneous way, and sometimes the images resurface later, by a roundabout route. But the fascination of these natural movements is probably appreciated by everyone, even if they did not grow up by a lake or in the middle of the countryside.

Tokujin is certainly familiar with the movements of wind and water, to which he alludes in some of his installations. For a window at Issey Miyake in Tokyo of 1997, he made a display consisting of snowflakes, represented by fine, downy feathers, with gusts of wind that whirled them back and forth. He showed a variant of the same design in the office of an advertising agency during the Cologne furniture fair (2002). I can imagine how the passers-by stood and stared in Tokyo, not only because they were surprised to see 'snow' in the hot Japanese summer, but also because of the mesmerising, continually changing formations of the flakes in the air.

One of my own designs went into operation in 2003 at the new Toronto airport. Inside a huge Plexiglas tank, small cubes – mostly transparent but with a few red and black exceptions – are catapulted around by a jet of water. Although the materials are quite different, the result is similar to the whirling snow. The water tank was originally planned as part of the architecture. Since the design was for an airport – and I myself spend a lot of time at airports – I deliberately set out to create something that would have a soothing, meditative quality.

The fascination of these seemingly random movements, following laws that the eye cannot grasp, can lead us to forget, at least momentarily, our next goal or the problems we are carrying around in our head. It allows us to relax mentally without really noticing the brief pause. That is why I gave the water tank an alternative title – 'Don't miss your plane!' – after it was finished. With the swirling water, like the snow in the shop window, there is a risk that the viewer will switch off for too long and miss his connection.

Tokujin's feathery snow also reminded me of one of my earliest visits to Japan, when I was taken to a traditional 'kabuki' theatre. In the early 1970s, 'kabuki' was almost unknown in Europe and America, except in specialist circles: to me, certainly, it was a name, but nothing more. During the performance, which featured a set and costumes in shockingly bright colours, snow – or was it flower petals? – suddenly began to float down from the flies above the stage. It was a truly beautiful moment, without even a hint of kitsch, and one that is hard to achieve.

One could probably point to influences of such traditional Japanese art forms or cultural techniques in Tokujin's work: for example, in his use of movements that occur in nature. But it is obvious that a person will be influenced by the culture of the country in which he grew up. Tokujin himself identifies relationships with Japanese traditions, as in the case of his TōFU lamp (2000), where, as he says, 'most of the work has gone into the preparation of the material', and the product itself looks very simple – a principle often seen in Japanese cuisine, from which it draws its inspiration.

The fascination of natural movements is universal. The movements of people in groups can also display this quality of randomness and apparent chaos, but there are few places where one can observe it. At the Shibuya station in Tokyo there is a 'scramble' crossing, where streams of pedestrians converge from all four sides, meeting and disappearing in the surrounding streets. The crossing is in an extremely busy area: the pedestrians pour onto it like a tidal wave when the traffic light turns green. I know of people who have stood there for ages watching the endlessly repeated movement. It is only a minor point, but I seem to remember that Tokujin's studio is not far away from this crossing.

I visited the studio of Tokujin Yoshioka Design last year, on an evening when it was raining. Long taxi rides in a city like Tokyo, as I sit gazing with tired eyes at the streams of pedestrians and the reflections of the lights in the wet streets, can sometimes upset my sense of direction. The building where Tokujin works is an old granary, a barn that he shipped to Tokyo from somewhere in the provinces, several hundred kilometres away, and renovated with modern materials. That is another thing I like about Tokujin: he neither fetishizes change nor puts too much emphasis on tradition – instead, he keeps the two aspects in balance and can link them in ways that seem natural and unforced. Change without movement – if only of the brainwaves – is scarcely conceivable. Movement (and the resultant change) is a sign of animation, proof that not everything is petrified, frozen and ultimately dead, or moribund. An environment such as a desert or an ice field, in which, at least to the untrained eye, there is no movement, strikes us as hostile to life itself.

Tokujin's designs inspire a great deal of interest: his moving objects are as attractive to exhibition visitors as to chance passers-by. In the touring Issey Miyake exhibition, Making Things (1998–2000), which I visited at the Fondation Cartier pour l'art contemporain in Paris, the garments were mounted on wire frames connected to sensors that moved the exhibits around, each following its own path. The children visiting the show provided the clearest example of how seeing movement can stimulate the viewer's own energies. However, it is not easy to use movement in exhibitions. Wrong or superfluous movements deflect the viewer's attention from the real theme: they appear forced or meaningless. Tokujin's results show that he always engages closely with the theme in question.

Very young babies, only a few weeks old, already pay attention to moving objects, trying perhaps to understand the rules that govern particular movements. Researchers have patiently mapped the movements of the planets in our solar system, which appear at a certain point to be slowing down. Understanding patterns of movement seems to be a basic human urge. Regular, predictable movements can be beautiful and can hold our attention for a while, but they eventually become insignificant, and are scarcely perceived; they can have a soporific effect like the pendulum of a grandfather clock, idly observed in a moment of boredom.

Irregular movements are inevitably more interesting. Wind and water are especially apt to produce movements that are unexpected, although there are physical laws that describe them. To the human eye, wind and water continually create effects that seem to be governed by chance and have a certain air of mystery. It is as if the unpredictability in the movement of clouds across the sky, or the shifting pattern of waves seen from the after-deck of a boat, were reflected directly in the viewer's thought processes. Ideas begin to drift away from their customary path and may suddenly take a new direction.

Water and air are essentially transparent, and transparency is a subject that has frequently interested Tokujin. Clear materials also have a mysterious character. They are there, and you see something, but then you don't. For example, in the recently completed Roppongi Hills development in Tokyo (2003), there is a chair that Tokujin calls Chair That Disappears in the Rain (2003), made entirely of glass. You think you see the object, but you could equally be looking at mere reflections or distorted images of the other objects round about. Sitting in the chair, you find yourself inspecting the forms with your hands.

Whereas water is visible, wind – or the movement of the air – can only be seen through the effect it has on visible objects. In the Hermès shop window in Tokyo, for a project called Air du Temps 90x90 (2004) there was a picture of a face with slightly inflated cheeks and pouting lips, and next to it a scarf that flutters gently in the surrounding air currents. Like all Tokujin's work, it is very simple and very effective, but also it seems to radiate a tremendous amount of human warmth. I find that I ask myself, and Tokujin, what movements and emotions would emerge if we could communicate directly in the same language?

Hermès Air du Temps 90x90

This project combined an exhibition and window installation at Maison Hermès in Tokyo. Featuring the Hermès collection of scarves, all to the same size of 90x90 cm, Tokujin wanted to show their beauty by recreating the movement of each as it is worn by a woman and sways softly in the air, in a fantasy world. The window is designed with the image of a woman projected onto the monitor (see previous page), with the scarf in front of her moving as she appears to blow. The concept continues inside with a large display of scarves filling the exhibition space.

Hermès Air du Temps 90x90, window installation and exhibition, 2004, Maison Hermès, Tokyo

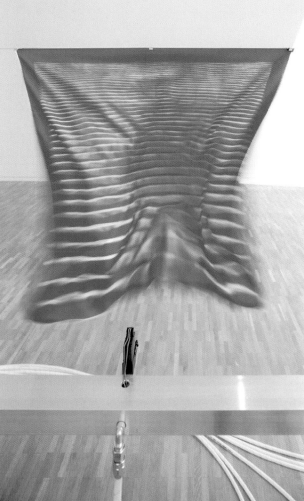

The space was filled with 48 air compressors, which
in turn made the scarves dance lightly in the air. Moving in
accordance with the sounds of the valves, the effect
was as if the sighs of 48 people were breathing life into them.

Hermès Air du Temps 90x90, window
installation and exhibition, 2004, Maison
Hermès, Tokyo

Issey Miyake
Making Things – Paris

This exhibition for Issey Miyake toured around three cities, Paris, New York and Tokyo. Made up of various installations, its basic concept was to express the garment-making process and to emphasize the unique characteristics of the clothes. In Paris, the show was held at the Fondation Cartier pour l'art contemporain, where it attracted an unprecedented number of visitors and was highly acclaimed globally.

Issey Miyake Making Things, touring exhibition, 1998–2000, Fondation Cartier pour l'art contemporain, Paris

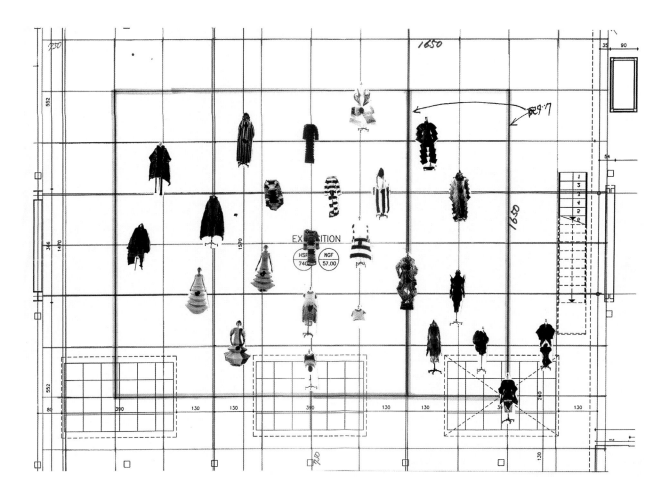

Issey Miyake Making Things, touring
exhibition, 1998–2000, Fondation
Cartier pour l'art contemporain, Paris

An installation called 'Jumping' featured sensors that were attached to the clothes, so that they moved comically in response to human movements (opposite).

Issey Miyake Making Things, touring
exhibition, 1998–2000, Fondation
Cartier pour l'art contemporain, Paris

Issey Miyake
Making Things – New York

Continuing the tour from Paris, the exhibition was held at the Ace Gallery in New York. As the installation was reinterpreted for the new space, the exhibition was revitalized. The futuristic clothes were displayed dramatically at the entrance, and in another zone the images showing the making process were projected onto the floor to magical effect.

Issey Miyake Making Things, touring exhibition, 1998–2000, the Ace Gallery, New York

Issey Miyake Making Things, touring
exhibition, 1998–2000, the Ace Gallery,
New York

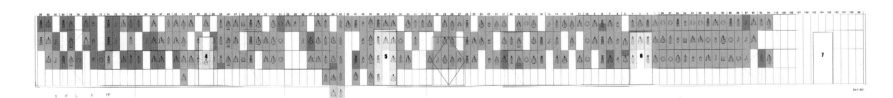

Issey Miyake Making Things, touring exhibition, 1998–2000, the Ace Gallery, New York

Issey Miyake
Making Things – Tokyo

After Paris and New York, the exhibition finished in Tokyo
at the Museum of Contemporary Art. It encompassed all the
main features of the previous two venues.

Issey Miyake Making Things, touring
exhibition, 1998–2000, the Museum
of Contemporary Art, Tokyo

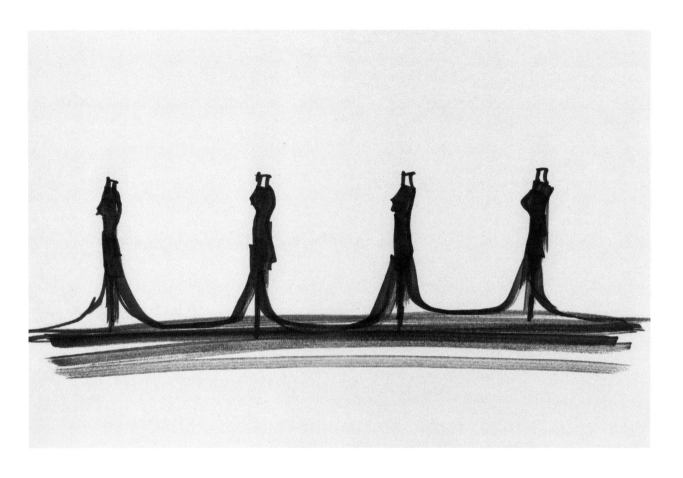

As the clothing line is based on the concept of one piece of cloth, the entire space was covered with an immense roll of material to emphasize the theme of garment-making.

Issey Miyake Making Things, touring exhibition, 1998–2000, the Museum of Contemporary Art, Tokyo

Issey Miyake Making Things, touring
exhibition, 1998–2000, the Museum
of Contemporary Art, Tokyo

Issey Miyake Snow

This window installation was based on the theme of 'white', the concept for the Paris collection of that year. The idea of snow was developed as a means of expressing this colour within the white interior of the boutique through movement rather than by construction. The 'snow' was suggested through using feathers, repeatedly blown upwards by a fan, that would dance in the air and pile upon the clothes. The effect was more dramatic for being shown in the middle of summertime.

Hermès

For this installation at Maison Hermès, the large glass window was showcased with a leather saddle and then a Kelly bag set in front of blown-up images of running horses. Tokujin recreated the motion caused by a horse running and a person walking to play with the idea of presence through objects – the saddle that leapt like a rodeo machine (opposite) and the bag that moved like a pendulum (below).

Hermès, window installation, 2002,
Maison Hermès, Tokyo

Muji+Infill Renovation

The concept for this interior for a typical Japanese apartment was to design 'nothing'. The result was not a conventional renovation but a proposal for a new vision of living. It involved redesigning a three-bedroom floor plan into one room by furnishing an entire wall with sliding and folding doors. Within the folding doors, every necessity of life is installed to meet the lifestyles of each resident. By opening a door, the room was transformed from a kitchen to a living room to an office. The project used a recycled wood, in which old wood chips and resin are synthesized, for a durable, seamless surface.

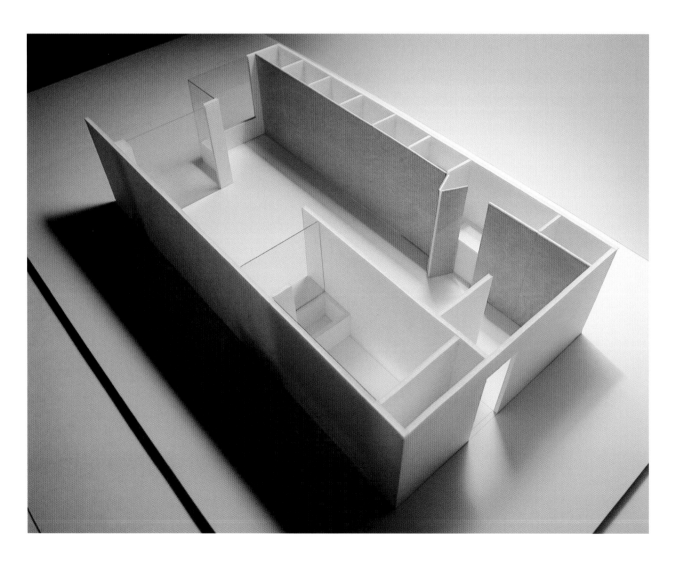

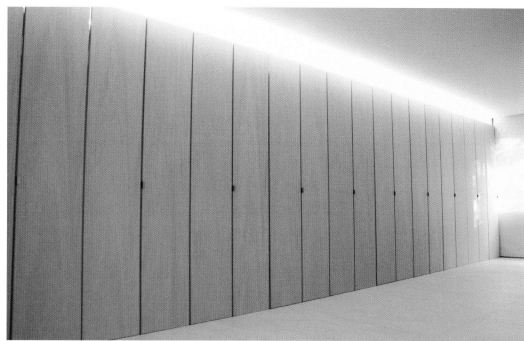

Muji+Infill Renovation,
interior, 2003, Tokyo

Transforming a Japanese Warehouse

For his own studio, Tokujin attempted to build a new architecture by appropriating an aged structure. Combining the values of the traditional building, a 'form born out of necessity', the aim was to use new industrial materials to create something of renewed value and interest.

Transforming a Japanese Warehouse, architectural project, 1999–2000, Shimane to Tokyo

Transforming a Japanese Warehouse,
architectural project, 1999–2000,
Shimane to Tokyo

For the project, a 150-year-old rice warehouse in the Shimane Prefecture was disassembled and relocated in its wooden framework in Tokyo.

The building presents many kinds of contrasts, the new versus the old, the natural versus the industrial, as a proposal for a new kind of architecture for the future.

Transforming a Japanese Warehouse, architectural project, 1999–2000, Shimane to Tokyo

Material

Before I had met Tokujin Yoshioka, I was immersed in his curious world at least twice. The first time, in 1998, I remember giggling with delight. This was the Making Things exhibition of Issey Miyake's work at the Fondation Cartier in Paris, designed and curated by Tokujin, and one of the best shows I have ever visited. In bursts of colour and light, Miyake's folded and pleated garments jumped up and down from the ceiling, as if they were excited to see us, and a big A-POC (A Piece Of Cloth) roll was being readied for the cutting. The exhibition toured and I saw it again at the Ace Gallery in New York some months later. The second time around, the effect was the same: mouths ajar, kids almost cartwheeling with the thrill of it all, and fun and surprises all over again.

The second time was when I visited Miyake's A-POC Aoyama, Tokyo (2000), which was devoted not to clothes, but rather to a system – the continuous textile extrusion A-POC, which Miyake conceived with engineer Dai Fujiwara. Although the space was detailed and beautiful, the interior design was elegantly selfless and the spatial attention devoted to process, to things in the making. The finished products on the racks were just examples, meant to show some possible applications. Letting customers interpret the material and finish their own design, with individuality and playfulness, is truly what A-POC is about, and Tokujin, with characteristic sensitivity, interpreted this concept in the space.

By the time I got to my third exposure, at the 2001 opening of the New Tokyo Lifestyle Think Zone in Roppongi, I had heard more about Tokujin, such as the fact that Shiro Kuramata and Issey Miyake were his mentors and that he trusted materials over forms. Feeling topsy-turvy, standing in the middle of the big Think Zone architecture on a floor that was a giant projection screen, the lights and shapes of the street outside deformed and refracted in a kaleidoscopic effect on the glass walls, I pondered the relationship between Tokujin and Kuramata, the late master of design for whom Tokujin worked, and Miyake, to whom Kuramata introduced him. I speculated that the element common to all three men, above and beyond their innovative instinct, their Japanese minimalism-with-a-twist, and all other benign stereotypes that they graciously bore, was trust.

Trust means controlling any process – becoming friends, becoming pupil to a master or master to a pupil, designing a space or an object – only up to a certain point, setting up the parameters for what is to come, and then letting go, allowing the body, the street, the world to take over the task of determining the shape. Trust, in the work of these three outstanding designers, has manifested itself most evidently in their passion for materials and for the inspiration that materials can provide. In 1996, just five years after his death, Kuramata's widow Mieko organized an exquisite show at the AXIS Gallery in Tokyo about the materials that had inspired her husband's work. Miyake loves new and old technologies and can distil from them the highest poetry, along with new ideas of beauty. And Tokujin is frequently quoted as having said: 'A concept [is] often inspired simply by the desire to use materials in a new way or process … I never start with form.' In his hands, paper, LEDs or dichroic film become structure and space, and what acrylic resin and metal mesh were to Kuramata, and pleats and new synthetic fabrics are to Miyake.

One of Tokujin's best-known designs, the Honey-pop chair (2001), is entirely made of a paper honeycomb similar to those used in decorative lanterns. The chair comes flattened, just like a lantern, and feels very fragile and ethereal. Once peeled open like an accordion and prepared, it accepts the impression of the first body that sits on it. The honeycomb cells in the superficial layer are compressed together and become a skin that confirms the chair's final solid state – and establishes a permanent stamp of ownership. Did Tokujin really design a chair, or is this the embryo of a chair? Next, Honey-pop becomes a fully fledged product when solidified in polyethylene and manufactured industrially by the Italian company Driade, who turn into a whole series under the name of Tokyo-pop (2002). It includes a couch, stools and little tables. Having fallen from the world of ideas, as they approach the ground, the design concepts acquire definition for commercial reasons.

The Honey-pop, like so many Tokujin designs, recalls the work of another master of playfulness and surprise: Bruno Munari. Were they still available, Munari's 'Travel Sculptures', made of foldable paper, would be on Tokujin's shelves and in his suitcase. And Munari, were he alive, would love many of the works by Tokujin, in particular the Chair That Disappears in the Rain perhaps, a glass outdoor bench – or the ghost of a bench – designed for the new Roppongi Hills area of Tokyo (2003). Chairs are the objects that embody everybody's conscious experience of design. For designers, they represent a ritual of initiation. In chairs more than in any other object, human beings are the unit of measure to which design must defer. In chairs, designers walk the fine line between standardization, imposing one form for all bodies for the sake of serial production, and personalization, accommodating each body in its exquisite individuality. In other words, chairs are a designer's obsession. How was Tokujin able to let go of so much, and achieve so much in return?

Because they are so apparently unintended, the forms that Tokujin produces come to us like a gift, and his useful objects promise and deliver emotion and surprise. They are the outcome of the designer's ability to tame the delight of the first creative idea by means of a rigorous discipline that will transform such an idea into something functional, understandable and available. The inspiration is sometimes odd, as in the TōFU lamp (2000), which is manufactured by imposing upon acrylic resin all the different steps normally used to produce tofu the food. The process is complex – it consists of repeated pourings into successive moulds, cooling, cutting, purifying and refining, before the light bulb is at last inserted – and leads in the end to the simplest and most understated form. In keeping with another cliché about Japanese culture, it is about obtaining the minimum apparent result with the maximum effort. The depth of the solution is evident to the trained eye.

Even more curious and telling than TōFU is the story behind Tokujin's own studio in Daikanyama, in the heart of Tokyo. The three-storey edifice is built on the wooden structure of an abandoned rice barn that Tokujin found in a completely different region of Japan, the Shimane Prefecture, and moved, truss by truss, to the city. In Tokujin's world, spaces not only have personalities, but also communicative souls. With this kind of approach, the notion of style is completely irrelevant and the work of a designer is akin to that of a writer, one who works first and foremost on the characters in order to build the narrative. There is no style, there is just invention, and every client and project demands a new one.

Tokujin does not have a style, but communicates joy in invention and in beauty, pleasure and humour, as well as pride in the display of his technical and constructive skills, at all scales of design. He studied interior design, but does not see any difference between that and furniture design or creative building restoration. His work revolves around his endless curiosity and restless exploration of materials so that they can become fluid forms, colours, textures – in other words, wavelengths.

Is design relevant, when we have so many big thoughts to think? Can a beautiful chair reach beyond its immediacy and be something more than just beautiful – and comfortable? Can a handsome space teach us something about life, and possibly inform our future actions in a positive way? The answer is, yes, sometimes. Some objects are designed from the inside out, soul and brain first. These contemporary objects reveal the history and radiate the material tradition that has shaped them, while at the same time speaking a global language. They display an intelligence of the future. Just like great movies, they spark a sense of belonging in the world, in these exciting times of cultural and technical possibilities, while also managing to carry us to places that we have never visited. Any designer who is able to present us with such an experience is adding something special to the world, and that designer is Tokujin Yoshioka.

Honey-pop

Perhaps Tokujin's most famous work so far, the Honey-pop
chair is part of the permanent collections of the Museum
of Modern Art in New York, the Vitra Design Museum
in Berlin, the Centre Georges Pompidou in Paris and the
Victoria and Albert Museum in London. The revolutionary
design uses an innovative process that produces a
delicate yet strong honeycomb-structured paper chair.

Honey-pop, chair, 2001, Tokujin
Yoshioka Design

Honey-pop, chair, 2001, Tokujin
Yoshioka Design

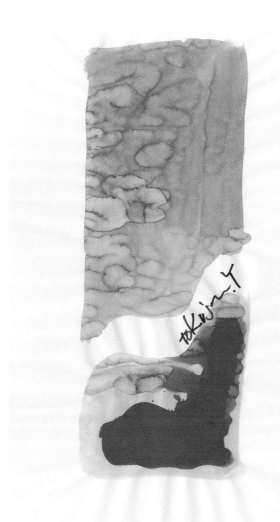

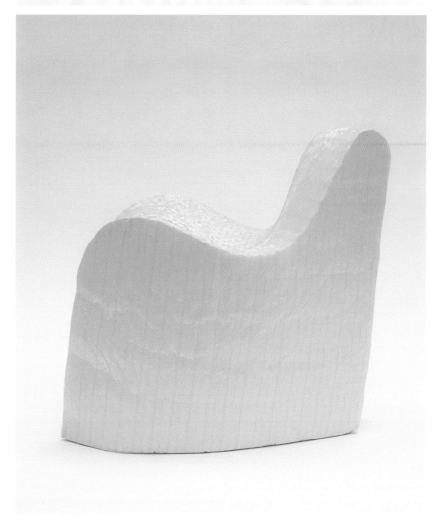

Tokujin shows each stage in the construction of the chair,
from cutting and unfolding to sitting. The chair is made up of
120 sheets of glassine paper, which are piled together to a
thickness of 1cm. Cut into appropriate shapes, the chair is then
opened outwards like an accordion. Eventually, the chair
becomes the structure itself, as it derives its design from the
beautiful form of the shape of the sitter.

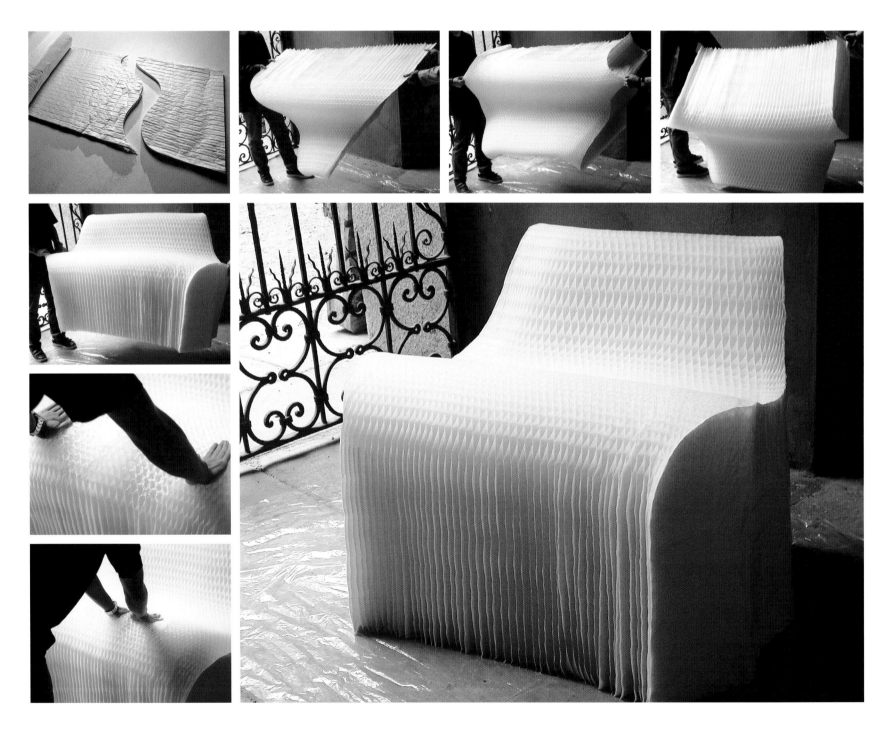

Honey-pop, chair, 2001, Tokujin
Yoshioka Design

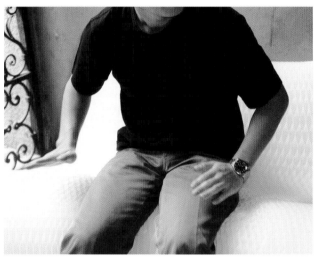

In 2002, Tokujin opened a workshop for primary school students at the MDS Gallery in Tokyo. Given the flat form of the honeycomb paper, the children were able to cut out the material easily to make hats for themselves.

Honey-pop, chair, 2001, Tokujin
Yoshioka Design

Tokyo-pop

Tokyo-pop is a furniture series for Driade based on the shape of the Honey-pop chair but mass manufactured using a cutting-edge moulded plastic technique. Such a 'pop' process allowed the creation of the chair in different sizes, from single to double, and as chaise longue. Available in different versions, to suit different lifestyles, it is produced in fabric as well as plastic and so is suitable for indoor or outdoor use.

Tokyo-pop, furniture, 2002, Driade

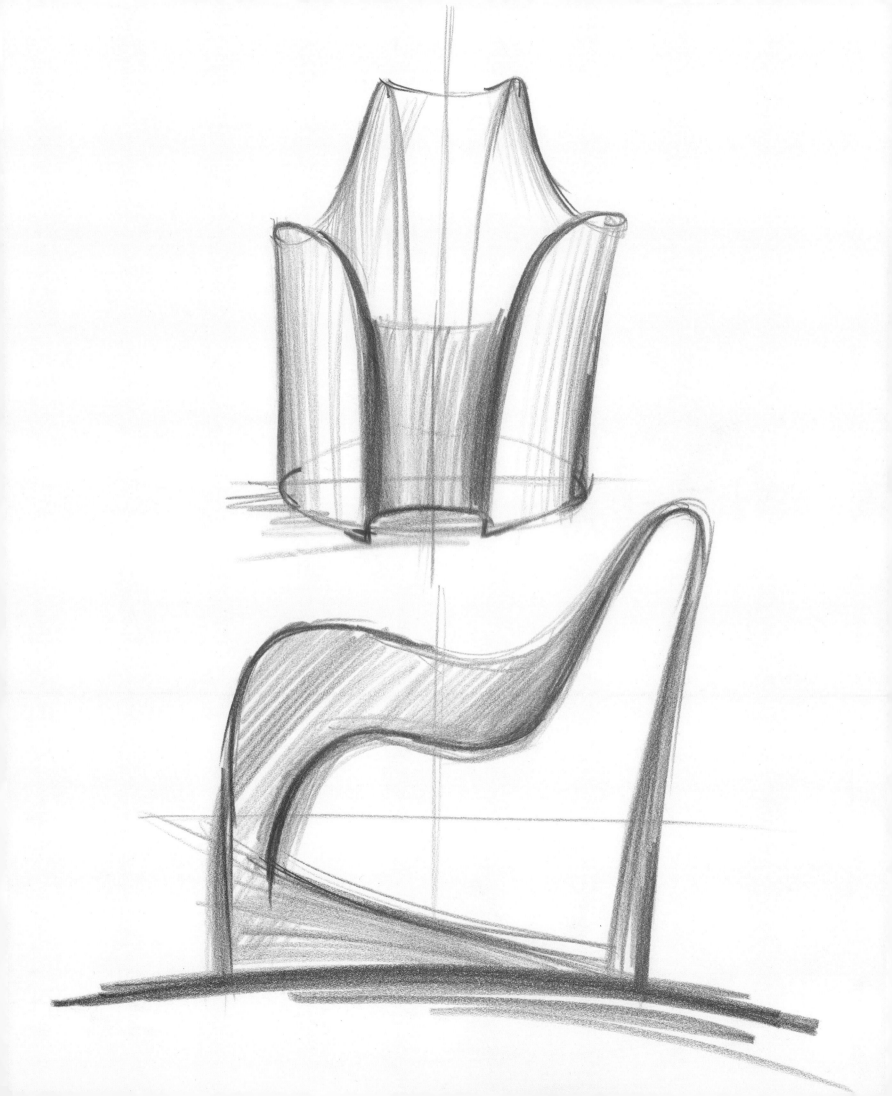

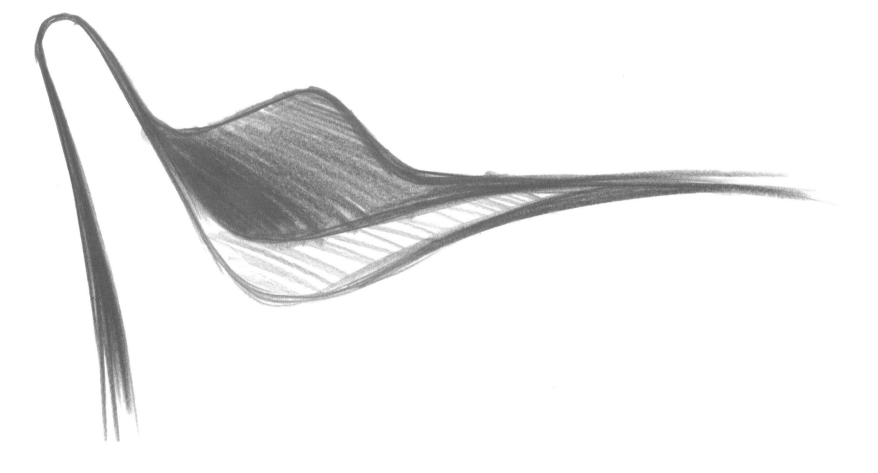

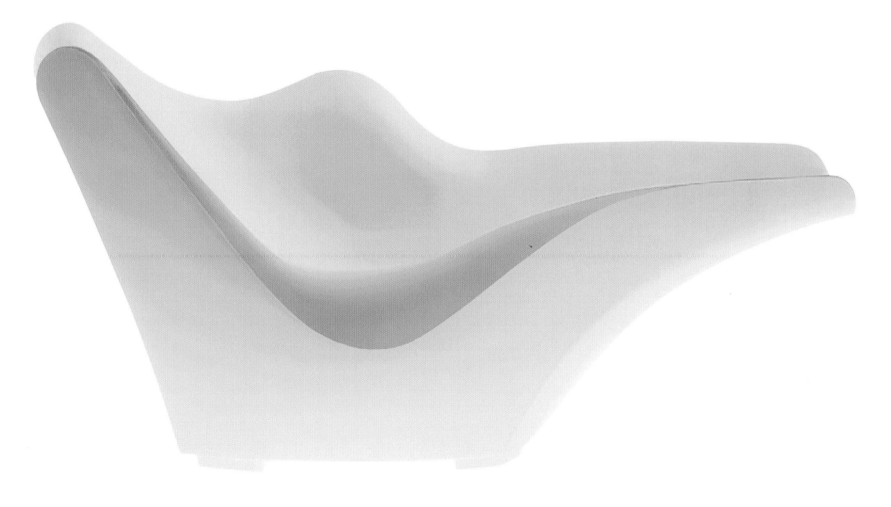

Tokyo-pop, furniture, 2002, Driade

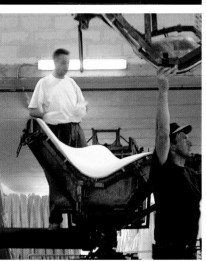

The sofa is completed through a method that is similar to making popcorn. Applying a technique of rotation moulding, the raw polyethylene pellets are loaded into a mould.

Tokyo-pop, furniture, 2002, Driade

Tokyo-pop was unveiled during an installation at dadriade in Milan, during the Salone Internazionale del Mobile in 2002, using the concept of a futuristic Japanese garden. The installation employed plastic pellets that are the raw material for Tokyo-pop. The space, covered with a considerable amount of pellets that corresponded to approximately 6,000 chairs, emphasized the sophisticated comparison of Japanese boldness and delicacy, and modern and traditional technology. At the end, the pellets were collected and recycled.

Tokyo-pop

Tokujin Yoshioka

Soft Boing

The concept was for a paper cushion made with aramid honeycomb, a special material used in aircraft wings and space shuttles. Chosen for its high elasticity, it enabled the creation of this paper sofa that functioned like a spring. It was then developed by Driade into a chair called Boing, using a pleated leather textile covering.

Soft Boing, chair, 2004, Tokujin
Yoshioka Design

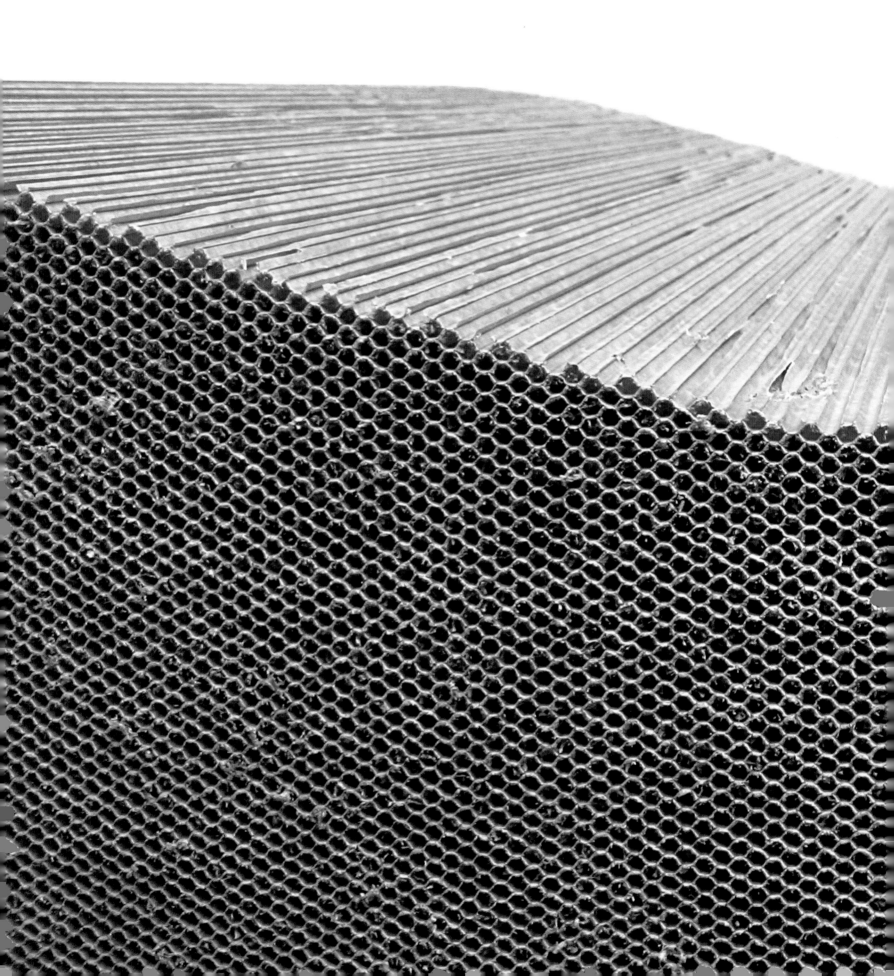

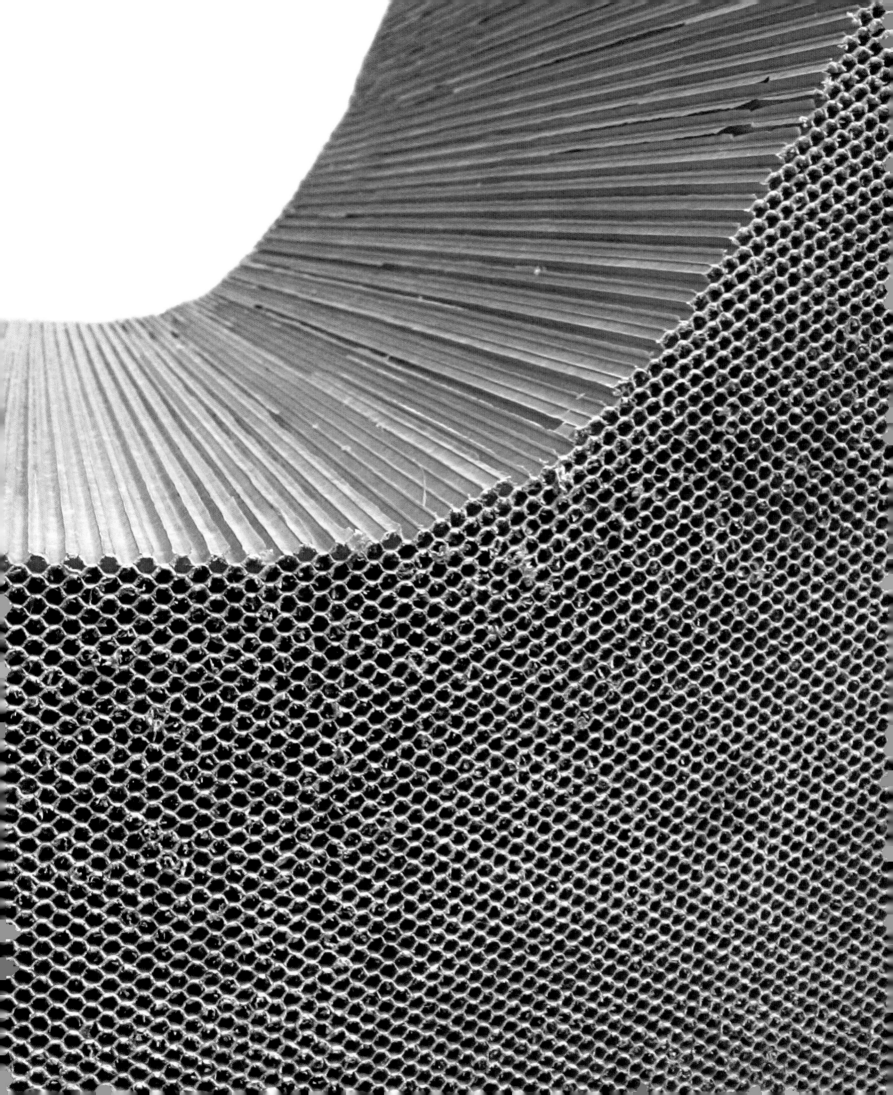

Boing

Boing was launched by Driade at the Salone Internazionale del Mobile in 2005. The series includes an armchair and sofa. Using innovative technology, the pleated leather covering creates air between the sitter's body and the chair to reduce friction or sweat. The result is a chair with such natural comfort that it functions almost like the surface of human skin.

Boing, furniture, 2005, Driade

A-POC

A-POC (A Piece Of Cloth) is a line of clothes by Issey Miyake created through a process analogous to moulding. For the shop interior, Tokujin was inspired by the function of a car's hydraulic and exhaust system as it resembled that of a building's ceiling ducts and other types of plumbing.

A-POC, shop interior,
2000, Aoyama

Dear Reader, Books by Phaidon are recognised world-wide for their beauty, scholarship and elegance. We invite you to return this card with your name and e-mail address so that we can keep you informed of our new publications, special offers and events. Alternatively, visit us at **www.phaidon.com** to see our entire list of books, videos and stationery. Register on-line to be included on our regular e-newsletters.

Subjects in which I have a special interest

☐ Art   ☐ Contemporary Art   ☐ Architecture   ☐ Design   ☐ Photography

☐ Music   ☐ Art Videos   ☐ Fashion   ☐ Decorative Arts   ☐ *Please send me a*
                                                                              complimentary catalogue

Mr/Miss/Ms   Initial   Surname

Name

No./Street

City

Post code/Zip code   Country

E-mail

This is not an order form. To order please contact Customer Services at the appropriate address overleaf.

Please delete address *not* required before mailing

PHAIDON PRESS INC.

180 Varick Street

New York

NY 10014

Return address for USA and Canada only

PHAIDON PRESS LIMITED

Regent's Wharf

All Saints Street

London N1 9PA

Return address for UK and countries
outside the USA and Canada only

*Affix
stamp
here*

In order to emphasize the A-POC concept in the shop, the casting process of recycled aluminium was used to cover the whole space.

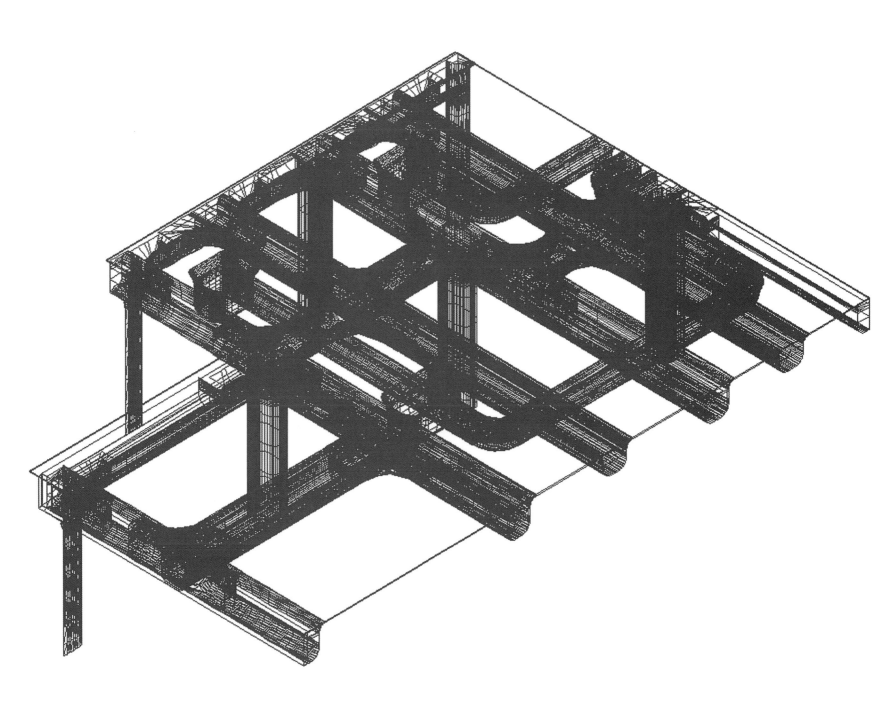

A-POC, shop interior,
2000, Aoyama

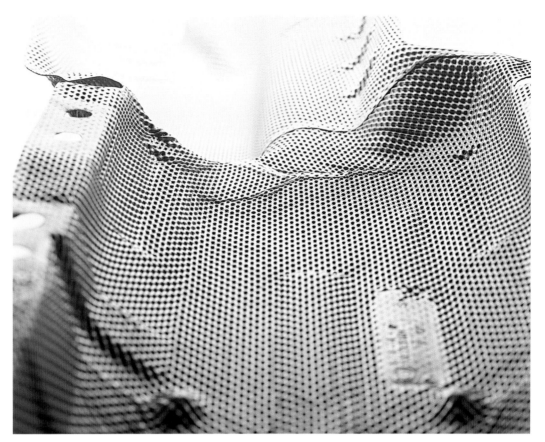

A-POC, shop interior,
2000, Aoyama

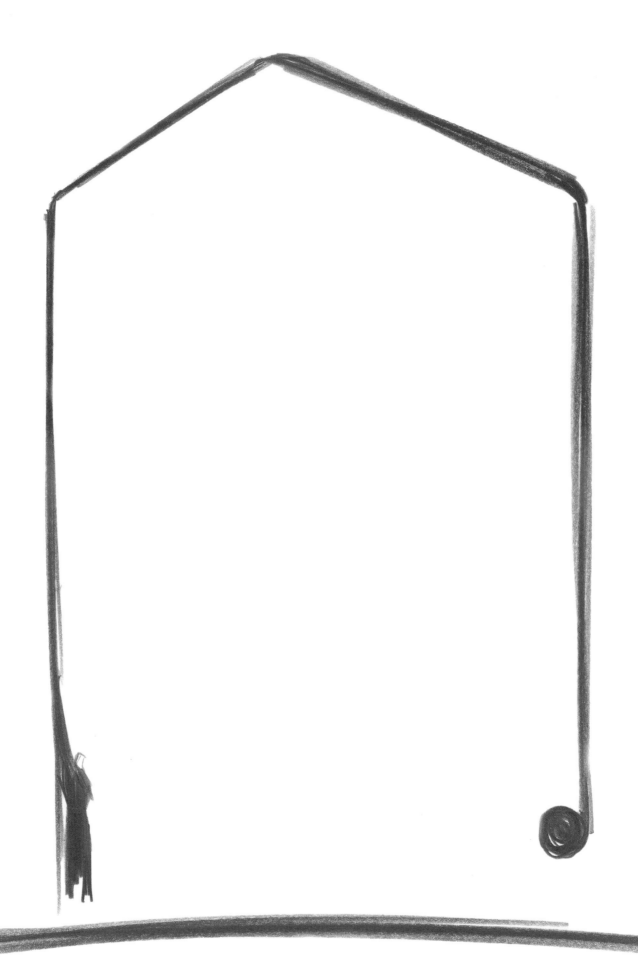

A-POC Making

This exhibition was held at the Vitra Design Museum in Berlin to present the A-POC (A Piece of Cloth) clothing line. For the installation, Tokujin transformed the long brick space that was once an electrical generation plant into a huge tunnel of colourful clothes.

A-POC Making, Issey Miyake and Dai Fujiwara, exhibition, 2001, Vitra Design Museum, Berlin

A-POC Making, Issey Miyake and Dai
Fujiwara, exhibition, 2001, Vitra Design
Museum, Berlin

The garments were exhibited at various stages in their
production to make reference to the unique 'tube moulding'
process with which they are created.

Media Skin

Since we have become increasingly in contact with our mobile phones, Tokujin's design for this product is based on the idea of assimilation, using a material that has the tactility of our skin. Like a 'second skin', the user and the phone become one entity as this mass-produced, hard product is turned into an object with emotional appeal, through its lightness and softness.

Media Skin, mobile phone concept, 2005, au design project for KDDI

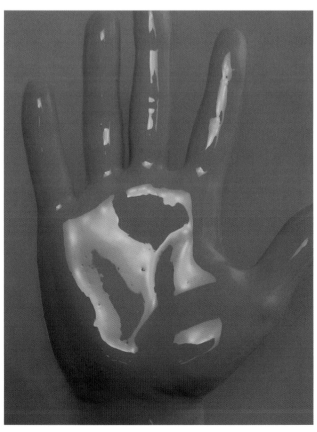

Media Skin, mobile phone concept,
2005, au design project for KDDI

Audi

This proposal for an Audi showroom takes the Audi car itself, with its composition of cast aluminium parts, as the basis for its concept. The plan uses liquid aluminium, melted at 700°celsius, and sprayed onto a curved surface, to create a seamless space. It is shown here as presentation model, in section, and to actual size (overleaf, after sketch).

Audi, showroom design, 2001, proposal

TO

Fascinated by the concept of creating a product from a single lump of metal, Tokujin's idea was to create a watch that is both timeless and that can tell the time. Initial concepts (overleaf, left) made use of LED screens on a wristband, which showed the time as an after-image. The final product, produced by Issey Miyake, is constructed as a flat surface inspired by the back of a watch. Incorporating the hour and minute hand, the result is an extremely simplified design.

TO, watch, 2005, Issey Miyake/
Seiko Instruments

ISSEY MIYAKE

TO, watch, 2005, Issey Miyake/
Seiko Instruments

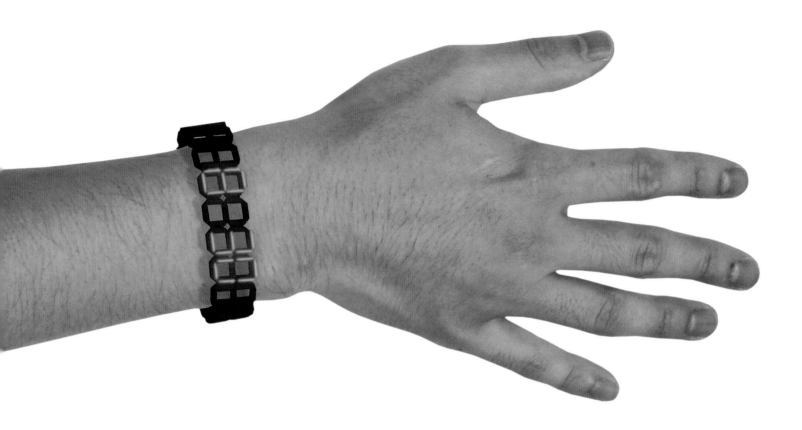

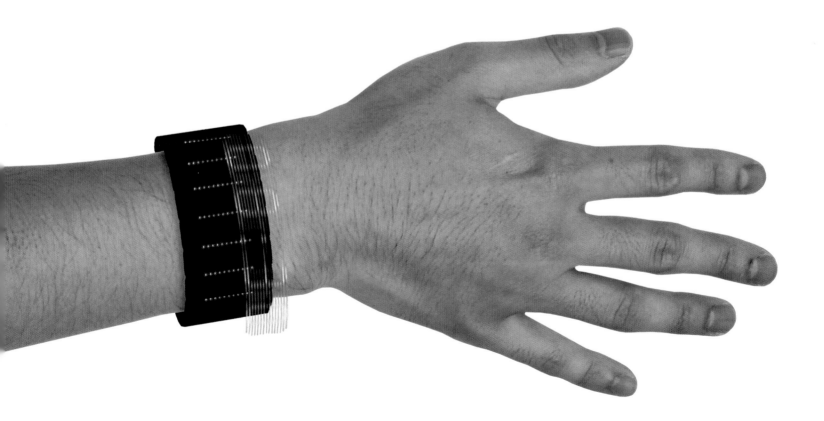

Light

The Inspiration of Tokujin
Kozo Fujimoto

The first time I encountered Tokujin Yoshioka was in 1998, when Issey Miyake introduced him to me as a young, but extremely talented, space designer. In the more than eight years of our acquaintance, I have had the good fortune to witness various projects in which he was involved. Beginning with Miyake's Making Things touring exhibition, at Fondation Cartier pour l'art contemporain in Paris (1998–2000), Tokujin has constantly invented challenging new schemes through exhibition-space construction, interior design, product design and event-space design. As if to counter his taciturn nature, he distinguishes himself through his perpetual ability to come up with daring and fresh surprises.

Prior to Miyake's introduction, I had no knowledge of Tokujin's work, and I was ashamed that I had failed to notice the existence of such an exquisite, talented designer so close by in Japan. Although many great Japanese designers were competing against one another at the time, very few were able to command attention on the international scene.

It is not an exaggeration to say that the world standard for interior-product design has centred on Western countries, as well as being established on occidental values. When distributing commodities in the world, religious and cultural differences derived from locality or ethnicity are ignored. Strategies of communication are obsessed with the global, not with difference, and in turn this is reflected in the manufacturing industry. Tokujin's design activities have, however, earned him a reputation within the growing focus on Japanese artistic culture in general (art, fashion, food, for example), which has resulted in a greatly increased understanding of Japan compared with a few years ago. Based on this high level of understanding, Tokujin has faithfully met expectations through his designs. Issey Miyake, as well as the late Shiro Kuramata, both of whom Tokujin admires as a pupil his teachers, have centred their design on the expression of the interior, a characteristic that is distinctly Japanese and which has had a huge impact on the Western world. Tokujin's designs, based on a unique modernity, continue their legacy.

In October 1999, Driade in Milan commissioned Tokujin to put forward an idea for a new product. His proposal did not begin with a handwritten drawing or plan, but with a concrete expression using computer graphics. The beautiful presentation, however, did not sufficiently convince Enrico Astori, president of Driade, to proceed with the project. Astori advised him, with regard to the issues that must be considered when creating commercial products, and told him he would wait for the next proposal. A year and half later, in April of 2001, Tokujin revisited Driade at the Salone Internazionale del Mobile with his new work, called Honey-pop. This design reflected his inherent perseverance and rare imagination, pointing to the source of his ability to imagine future possibilities.

Two people take the short ends of a piece of pleated paper, around 82 cm (length) x 92 cm (width) x 1 cm (thickness) and cut it out in the shape of a chair. It makes a hard, dry sound as they expand the pleats to about one metre, then reduce them again until the object makes an adequate seat, which they place on the ground. Tokujin sinks his buttocks into the bellows part of the chair, which resembles a fully expanded accordion, skilfully creating a comfortable sitting surface. This was the moment when the Honey-pop chair was born into the world, presented by Tokujin to Astori at the furniture shop dadriade on Via Manzoni, Milan. The fortunate visitors who happened to be present at this moment gathered around in a large crowd, voicing their admiration at the impromptu performance and firing questions at Tokujin. He also won the approval of the influential design magazine editors at this time, for this portable armchair made from strong paper. Although it was never mass-produced, it left an indelible mark on the history of design as the starting point of Tokujin's later product design.

In 2002, Tokujin presented through Driade the Tokyo-pop series, inheriting the idea of Honey-pop but manufactured in polyethylene in a single-body shape. To launch this product, the entire shop was covered in artificial snow, creating a beautiful effect that was the talk of the town. In 2003, he presented Tokyo-pop 2 (evolved from Tokyo-pop), as well as producing the exhibition for the thirty-fifth anniversary of Driade. In 2004, he went on to make the 'invisible' chair, Kiss Me Goodbye. This brought together several of the ideas that epitomized his activities. His insistence on 'invisibility' rather than transparency, which was a fantasy he had nurtured for some time, was supported by his spirited desire to overcome the impossible. He strove to achieve in his finished product a result that would differ from any transparent object previously created by designers in the past. In other words, he repeatedly polished the shaped product in an attempt to materialize the dream of invisibility.

In 2000, the Japanese company Yamagiwa manufactured Tokujin's lighting equipment, TōFU. One can say without exaggeration that he designed here not simply the object, but the expression of light itself. The moment the light is switched on, the effect surpasses the objective of illumination, flaunting the beauty of light. Transmitting light through a solid, transparent lump of acrylic, Tokujin transforms the way it moves, or how we perceive its conditions, since its behaviour inside the block is different from the way it reacts in the air. This object was an antithesis to fluorescent light, which had flooded dark, post-war, Japanese society in an attempt to encourage optimism. Although it does not reach the level of brightness or luminosity achieved by this, Tokujin's light object impresses its existence upon the mind; it cannot go unnoticed, and arouses a philosophical rethinking of the meaning of light.

In September 2003, Tokujin proposed an exhibition, again on the theme of light, for the launch of a new mechanical watch by Hermès, held at the University of Tokyo Museum, the oldest existing Western-style building in Japan. By covering all the windows in the building with an orange film, which filtered the natural light, he created a surreal, mysterious and nostalgic atmosphere. This very simple, beautiful solution seemed to arrest the present moment. As the light changed from afternoon to evening, then to night, Tokujin himself, clad in a white coat, added to the performance by pouring into a large glass container two kinds of liquid that transmit light when combined. The result was sheer surprise; he created dazzling light itself. The liquid coloured the room red and yellow and white, illuminating the new product on certain areas of the display shelves. The hall reverberated with a hubbub of admiration. This was exactly the effect he had planned. The new experience of light and shadow imbued the participants with a shared sense of exhilaration in this installation, called Hermès new watch Dressage.

In October 2001, Tokujin agreed to do two projects for Maison Hermès, a building made entirely from glass blocks and designed by Renzo Piano in Ginza, Tokyo. One was to design a photographic exhibition for the gallery space; the other was to decorate the display window facing the street. The exhibition (in 2002) comprised around thirty works by the Italian photographer, Fulvio Cinquini, who captures through his camera the interaction between horses and people around the world. Tokujin's proposal was to reinvent the space as a field through which horses gallop, creating a feeling of oneness with the animals through the use of sound. Bang & Olufsen provided several dozen free-standing speakers, and the space was filled with the sound of hooves and whinnying. The two display windows, on the other hand, featured a single object per window. In the first, a saddle was installed on a moving pedestal, creating a natural motion like that of a real horse. The other window featured a Kelly bag that swung like a pendulum.

In May 2004, Tokujin again worked with Maison Hermès, arranging Hermès scarves to the size of 90x90 cm in the gallery space and the display window (Air du Temps 90x90). The window display wonderfully expressed the movement of a scarf, as it swayed to the rhythm of human breath, suggested by a picture of a face that appears to be blowing, and executed by wind machines. People passing the windows stopped to gaze at the perfectly synchronized movements, taken in by the repeated actions. In the gallery, more than forty scarves were hung throughout the space, each moving according to random bursts of air, so that the whole resembled a live animal. In this way, one could experience the scarves in the same way one does when they are worn, their lively designs constantly changing into new forms.

Tokujin's opus of creative activities is a series of surprises, leaving vivid impressions on people's minds. The primary reason for this is his fresh imagination, and his refusal to repeat the same concept twice. His works speak of the extraordinary amount of time and energy he pours into the process of achieving the creative spark. When he says to his commissioners, 'I have a good idea', we can safely assume that it will already be close to the finished state, that he will have estimated to perfection the effect and outcome that his method will bring. He always draws out an answer that far surpasses the expectation of the client, never failing to impress. Supported by his self-awareness and self-confidence as a professional, Tokujin's pioneering quest to shape a new era is unstoppable. We are filled with the desire to entrust the unknown future into his hands, because he is already halfway there.

Tokujin's unflinching, large-scale imagination is the product of a rare genius. It has always been and will continue to be a Herculean task to convince the public through unique expression. However, that is precisely where he shows his genius. Many others are able to make good use of a restrained expressive element, but he never fails to stamp the 'Tokujin Yoshioka' identity within his extremely limited methodologies. His notion of beauty has raised the bar for other designers who wish to win the same level of approval. He preserves both his own individuality and a sense of the Japanese. It is an undeniable fact that he has released design from occidental values, added a new vocabulary, and continues to provide the world with new standards of design. My hope for Tokujin is not only that he will create new products, but that he will also propose a new statement for the future.

TōFU

As its name implies, this lighting product takes its inspiration from Japanese cuisine. At the basis of the TōFU concept is the immense amount of work that goes into the preparation of the material, in order to create as simple and pure a result as possible. In this case, the effect is as if Tokujin has designed not a light fixture, but light itself. In 2005, TōFU became part of the permanent collection of the Museum of Modern Art in New York.

TōFU, lighting, 2000, Yamagiwa

After initial various presentation ideas for different lighting fixtures (right), the final TōFU design was established. For the manufacture of the lamp, a similar pouring and setting process is used as for making tofu, until it is finally cut into square pieces, after which the light source is added to each piece.

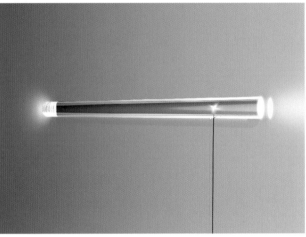

TōFU, lighting, 2000, Yamagiwa

Motion Graphics

In this exhibition, an extraordinary space was created whereby the whole floor served as display screens instead of using conventional video monitors. The mirror set up in the ceiling enabled the projection on the floor to double its size. In this way, Tokujin pushed the definitions of space design into a new direction.

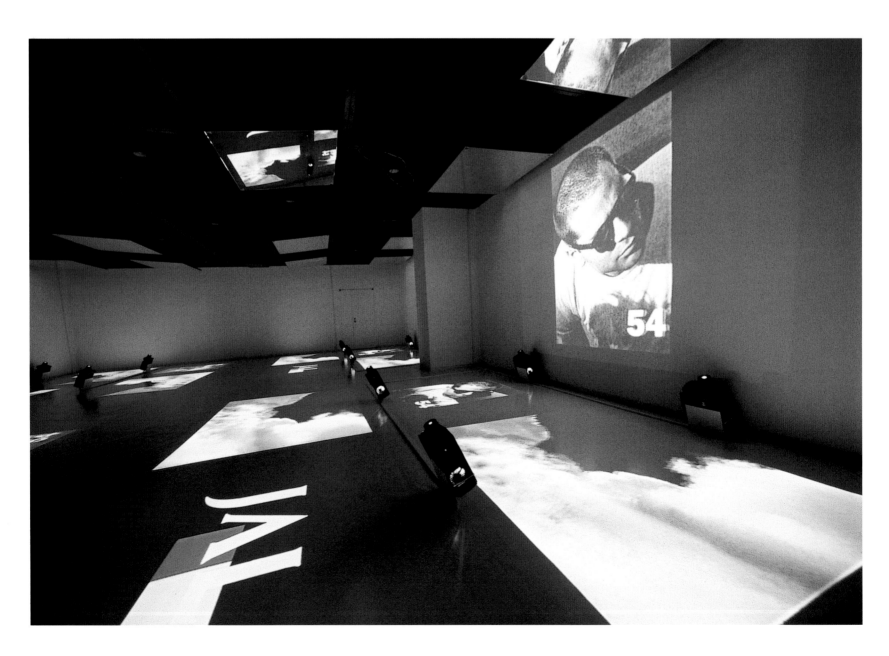

Motion Graphics, exhibition, 1997,
AXIS Gallery, Tokyo

Issey Miyake, shop interior,
2001, Kobe

Issey Miyake – Kobe

The theme for this shop interior is transparency, to symbolize
and convey a sense of the future. Instead of composing a
space simply with glass walls and acrylic furniture, Tokujin
attempted to create a space that would make the viewer
aware of its transparency through contrast with the opaque.
The walls look like translucent skin due to the use of lighting
tubes derived from fibre-optic technology.

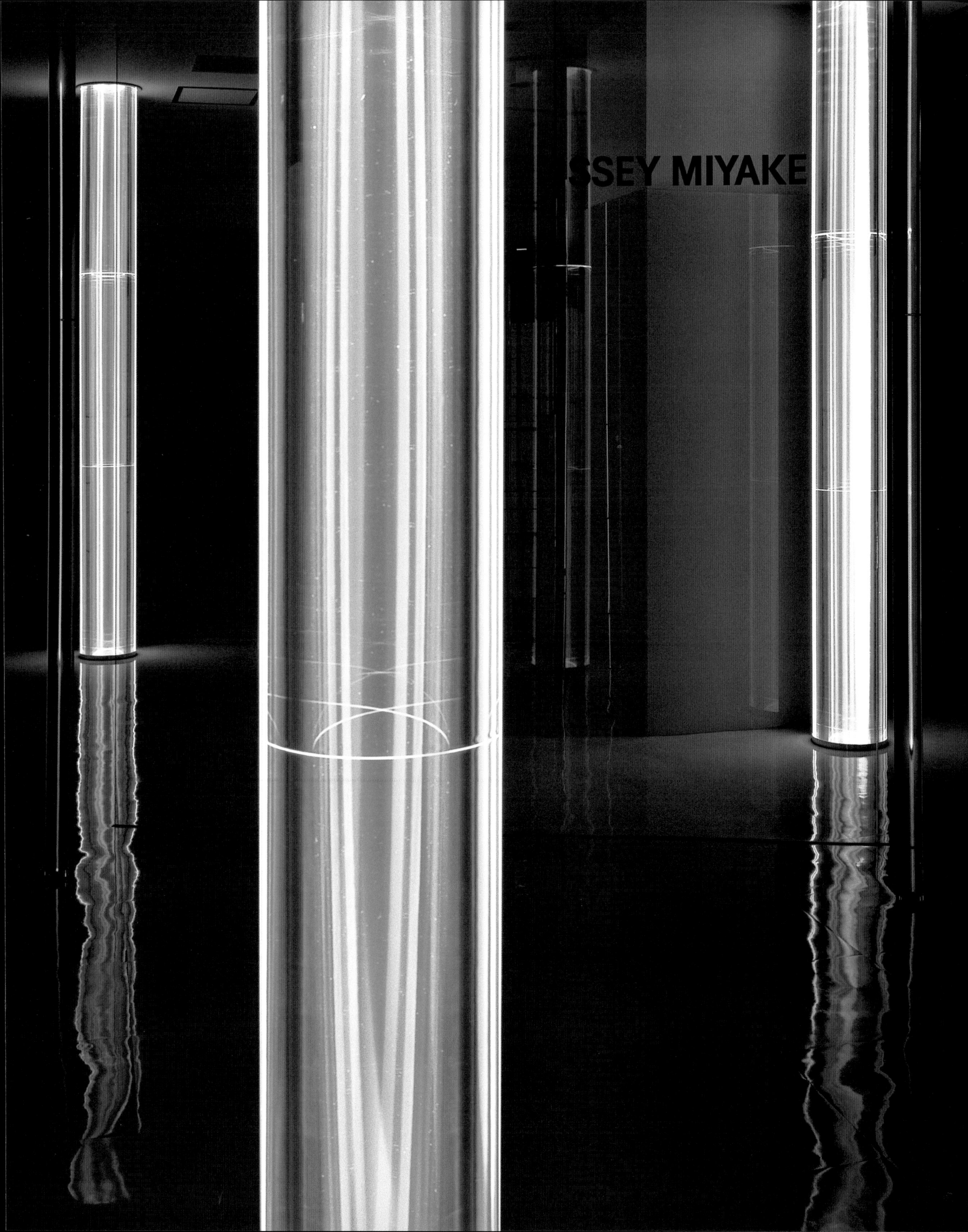
SEY MIYAKE

NTT-X

For this office space, Tokujin adopted an 'optical cable' that ran across the ceiling throughout the building to express the future values of the company. The lighting tubes, derived from fibre-optic technology, were used as a means of emphasizing the advance of the IT and Internet business. This office for a state-of-the-art business was created within an old building dating from 1958.

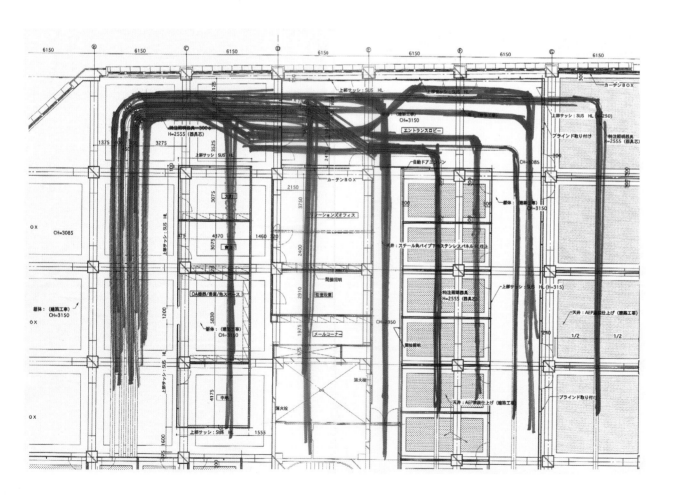

NTTX, interior, 2000, Tokyo

Peugeot Métamorphose

This installation was produced for a one-day event to celebrate the national debut of Peugeot 307cc. The theme was based on the 'métamorphose' of the coupe into the cabriolet. Using advanced technology, a series of movements of programmed lights on a huge wrap-around LED netting were created to express the image of visible wind. This was combined with music to create a total experience generating the best synergetic effect for the moving lights.

The LED netting was over 48.6 m long and was used
to surround the whole space. The concept emphasized
the significance of LED being introduced into the rear lamp
of the 307cc model for the very first time.

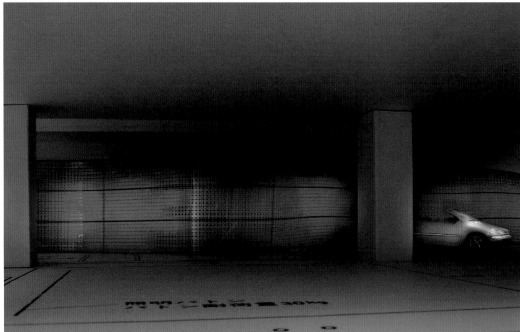

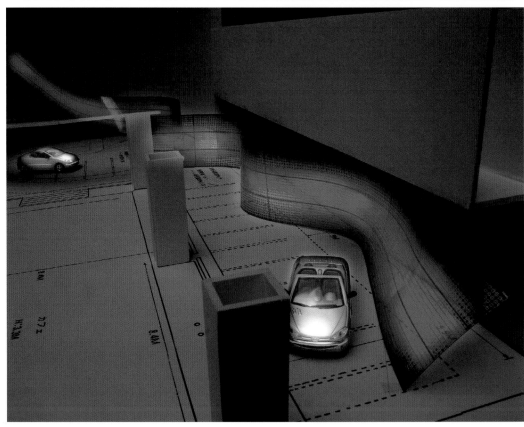

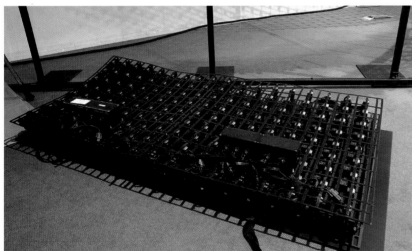

Peugeot Métamorphose, installation,
2004, Spiral Garden, Tokyo

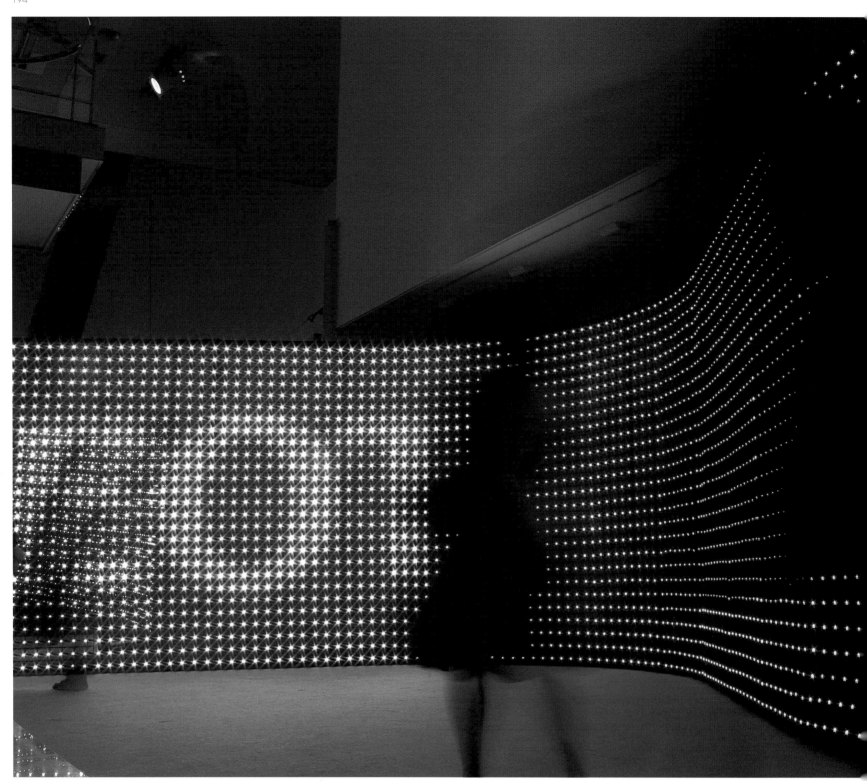

Peugeot Métamorphose, installation,
2004, Spiral Garden, Tokyo

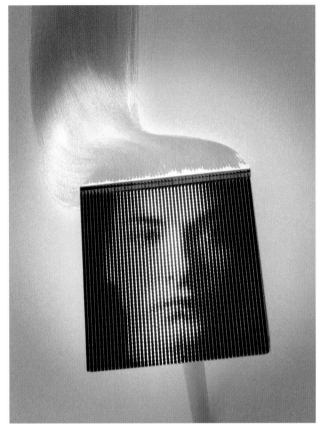 

Stardust

This unconventional chandelier, produced in collaboration
with Swarovski, is inspired by an earlier design for a table
called Capelli (above left), produced by Tokujin at the age of
24, which projected images through the use of fibre optics.
The new chandelier, made up of crystals, conjures up ideas
of a scene where moving images are projected onto the
night sky filled with the sparkling light of countless stars,
to present us with the vision of an exciting new future.

Stardust, chandelier and exhibition, 2005,
Swarovski Crystal Palace, Segheria
Gallery, Milan, and Meiji Memorial Picture
Gallery, Tokyo

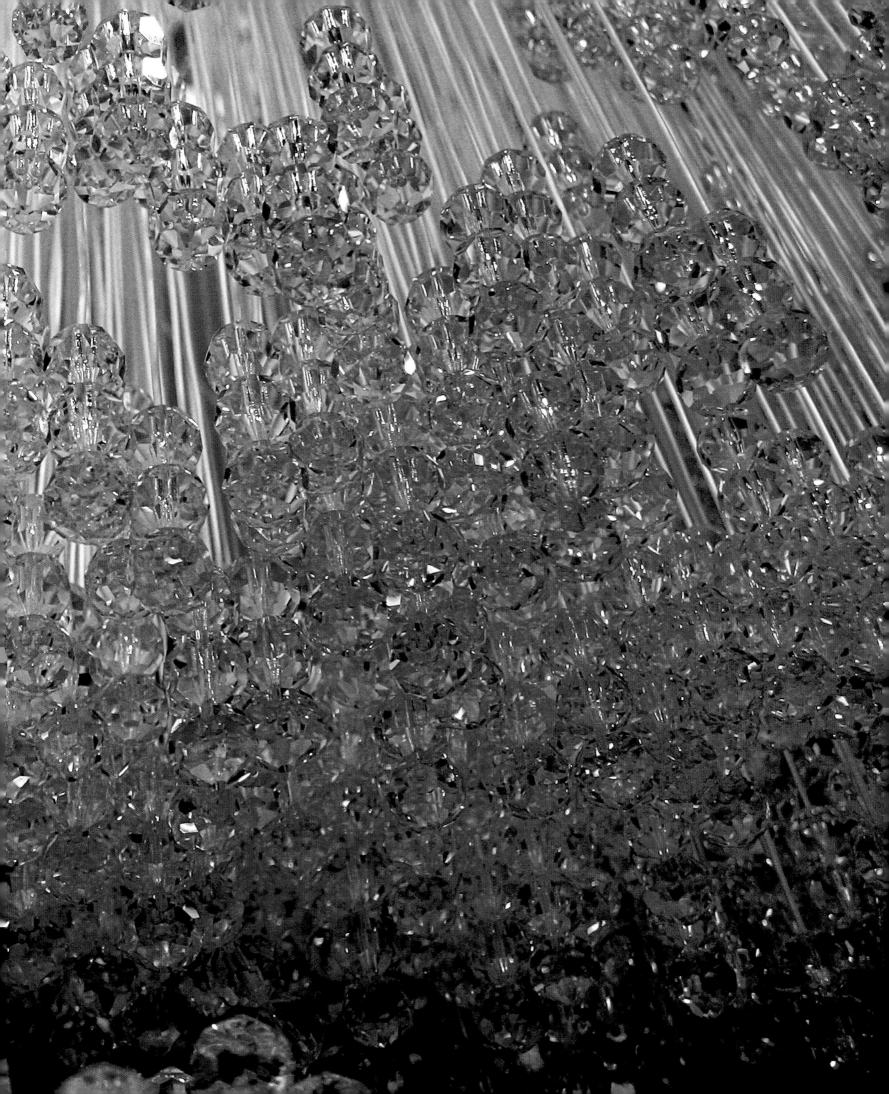

Using approximately 20,000 crystals on the tip of about 5,000 optical fibres, each functions as an image terminal. The chandelier was launched in Milan as part of the Swarovski Crystal Palace collection. In Tokyo, a similar version was featured as part of Tokujin's solo exhibition, with a 35-boy choir holding small lights to represent the crystals.

Stardust, chandelier and exhibition, 2005, Swarovski Crystal Palace, Segheria Gallery, Milan, and Meiji Memorial Picture Gallery, Tokyo

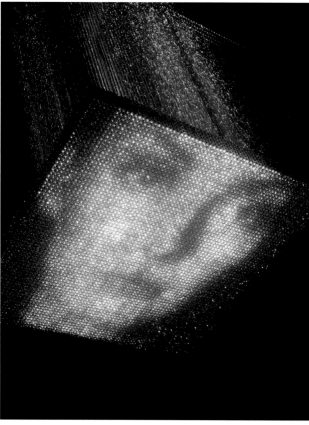

Profile
Tokujin Yoshioka

Career

1967	Born in Japan
1986	Graduated from Kuwasawa Design School
1987	Studied design under the late Shiro Kuramata
1988	Studied design under Issey Miyake
2000	Established Tokujin Yoshioka Design in Tokyo

Major Awards

1997	JCD Design Award
2000, 2001	ID Annual Design Review
2001	A&W Award – The Coming Designer for the Future
2002	Mainichi Design Award 2001
2005	Talents du Luxe 2005

The Honey-pop chair is in the permanent collections of the Museum of Modern Art, New York, the Vitra Design Museum, Berlin, the Centre Georges Pompidou, Paris, and the Victoria and Albert Museum, London.

www.tokujin.com

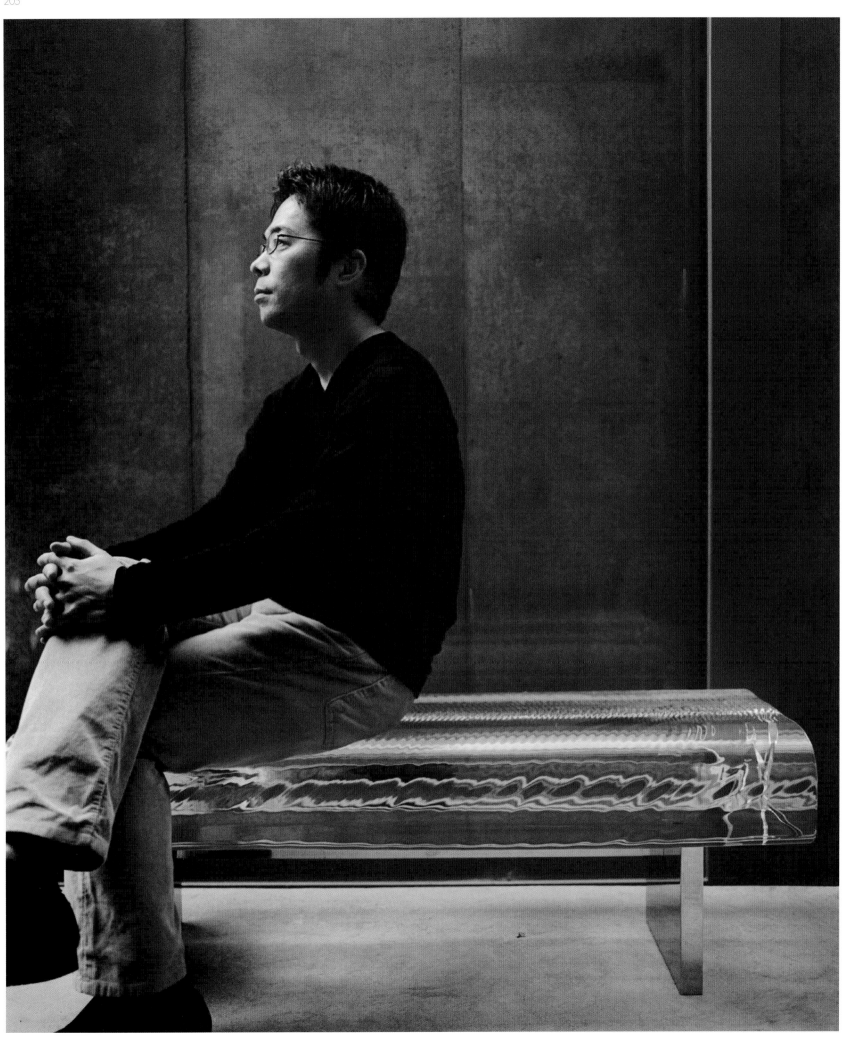

Index

Credits

Picture Credits

Unless otherwise stated below, images are provided courtesy of Tokujin Yoshioka Design: Shigeo Anzai: p10: Satoshi Asakawa: pp108, 109: Ryota Atarashi: pp118t, 119, 120: Philippe Chancel: pp87, 90r, 91: Robert Fischer: p16l: Mitsumasa Fujitsuka: p12: Masayuki Hayashi: pp18r, 30, 151t: The Issey Miyake Foundation: p20, 88l+br, 89bl+br: Jun Kumagai: p41: Mori Building: p54–5: Noboru Morikawa/ ELLE DECO Japan, No. 50: pp115, 118bl+br: Martin Müller, Berlin: p46: Atsushi Nakamichi/ Nacása & Partners Inc.: pp1, 7, 9r, 13, 14–15, 19r, 22l, 29, 33, 37, 38, 39, 40, 42–3, 45, 47, 74–5, 82–3, 84, 85, 106–7, p130tl, 141, 147tr, 151b, 152–3, 166–7, 181, 182, 183, 185, 187, 188–9, 196–7, 203: John Ross: p1: Seiko Instruments: pp169, 172: Hiroyuki Tachibana/ high fashion: p11: Kei Takashima/ Nacása & Partners Inc.: p202: Enrico Suà Ummarino: pp146, 147b: Tom Vack: p137: Yamagiwa: p178: Masahito Yamamoto: p177: Shin-ichi Yokoyama/Esquire Japan, July Issue: p205: Masaya Yoshimura/ Nacása & Partners Inc.: p57: Yasuaki Yoshinaga: pp8, 91, 86, 90l, 92, 93, 95, 96–7t, 98, 99, 102–3, 155, 156, 157r.
Cover image by Atsushi Nakamichi.

t=top, b=bottom, l=left, r=right

Acknowledgements

I would like to thank Richard Schlagman for giving me a wonderful opportunity to publish this book. I would also like to thank Emilia Terragni and Zoe Antoniou of Phaidon for their effort to put this experimental creation together, which, I believe, will challenge the publishing industry. Thank you so much to John Simpson of SEA Design for his beautiful graphic work. I am greatly touched by his sensitive creativity.

Respect and gratitude for Issey Miyake for his support over the years and understanding whenever I challenge new things. He has always given me higher hurdles to jump and I sincerely appreciate him for bringing me up through a number of projects.

I would also like to express my special gratitude to Elisa Astori, Ryu Niimi, Ross Lovegrove, Ingo Maurer, Paola Antonelli and Kozo Fujimoto, whose words have certainly become my valuable things. I still cannot believe that I have been given reviews from those I admire and respect very much. I have learned a new value of the design world through their works, which has always stimulated my own creation.

Many of my projects were presented through Atsushi Nakamichi's incredible photographs and I would like to gratefully thank him for reinterpreting my works with his own perspective.

My gratitude goes to all the craftsmen, collaborators, and staff, Reiko Ikehata, Takayuki Urata, Akira Nakagomi and Maki Izawa, who have worked and experimented together with me. Lastly, my special gratitude goes to Yoshiko Shimada for her hard work to publish this book.

Tokujin Yoshioka

Phaidon Press Limited
Regent's Wharf
All Saints Street
London N1 9PA

Phaidon Press Inc.
180 Varick Street
New York, NY 10014

www.phaidon.com

First published 2006
Reprinted 2010
© 2006 Phaidon Press Limited

ISBN 978 0 7148 4397 1

A CIP catalogue record of this book is available
from the British Library.

Designed by SEA

Printed in Hong Kong